Ten Reasons Why Africa Will Never Win the World Cup

by
Basil John Mandy

PublishAmerica

Baltimore

© 2005 by Basil John Mandy.

First printing

ISBN: 1-4137-4960-7
PUBLISHED BY PUBLISHAMERICA, LLLP
www.publishamerica.com
Baltimore

Printed in the United States of America

11th July 2005

Irene,

Thanks a lot for your interest in my book. I do appreciate it.
(Hope you enjoy it)

Best wishes, John.

Introduction

"The bicycle is the most civilised conveyance known to man. Other forms of transport grow daily more nightmarish. Only the bicycle remains pure in heart."

—Iris Murdoch, writer (1919-1999)

This book is not about football, and I apologise to anyone who has been deceived by the cover. The title is a reference to the famous prediction made by Pele that an African team would win the World Cup before the end of the twentieth century. As it turned out, he was wrong—an African team hasn't even been close, and these days most football fans would probably agree that an Asian tiger will win it before an African lion.

Pele's optimism was based on more than the simple fact that Africa has produced some of the world's most talented players. It was a reflection of the progress which he felt had been made in combating some of the horrendous problems that beset the continent. His premise was simple—Africans will overcome poverty, political instability, disease, and racial tensions. They will create a decent infrastructure and unleash the flair and enthusiasm of their footballers. They will win the World Cup. Like a million others, I was happy to buy into Pele's prediction. Then I rode the length of Africa on a bicycle and I changed my mind.

To my dismay, I found little evidence of genuine progress and in some important aspects I got the impression that Africa is going backwards. Today I think that African teams will continue to cause upsets because their players are so gifted, but not one of them is capable of going all the way to lifting the Jules Rimet trophy because there is something uniquely wrong with Africa. Great ingredients and the best oven in the world but the cake is a soggy, inexplicable mess.

My adventure was conceived during a weekend break in Paris with my wife, Joy, when we met a German called Heinz Sturke in a street market. I had read about Heinz in a cycle magazine and his life story had really caught my imagination. At fifty-seven years old, he has spent his entire adult life cycling around the world. He showed me a letter from the Guinness Book of Records confirming that he has ridden a bike to more countries than anyone else—every country in the world bar two, neither of which I had heard of. He had plans to tick them off and by now I am sure he has done so.

I have always had a hankering to go travelling and of all the various forms this can take, I wanted to do it on a bicycle. You can be almost completely independent on a bike—you don't need petrol, don't need to be an expert mechanic and you can forget about timetables. You decide when you start and when you stop. You travel at the speed you choose and even when your bike breaks you can always push it, although fixing it will never be much of a problem and will never cost much. Travelling on a bike means that you don't need to worry about what travellers worry about most—their transport.

Heinz could talk for England (or at least for Germany) and I listened to his stories and advice until eventually Joy's body language told me she had heard enough. A lot of what Heinz talked about was hardly rosy—the problems associated with getting food and water, flies, disease, crime, the loneliness. You go twenty-four hours without water in the desert and you are dead—could be a problem for someone with zero planning skills. Joy assumed he had put me off for good but to me it all sounded irresistibly attractive. As we tramped the streets of Paris I jabbered on about life on a bike and eventually Joy turned to me and said that if it was so important, now was as good a time as any to go. Getting the green light from Joy took me to another plane but I had the sense to realise that now was also as good a time as any to shut up about the subject. It was our wedding anniversary after all.

That was a Sunday afternoon and on the following Monday morning I was in my boss' office asking if I could have a year's leave of absence. We discussed the various arrangements I would need to make to cover my job and the effects on my contract of employment. Only after he had agreed in principle did he ask me what I planned to do with my year. Explaining that I wanted to cycle from Manchester to Cape Town, I saw for the first time the expression that was soon to become quite familiar. It said, You're obviously barking mad but I'm going to make a big effort and pretend you're sane.

Within a month, I had had all the jabs and inoculations I needed. I think there were a total of eleven diseases from which I was either given immunity or some degree of protection. In addition I got a year's supply of Larium, the very powerful but unpleasant anti-malaria drug. It has about a dozen side effects and I experienced most of them. A girl at work who had travelled extensively in third world countries gave me a little medical bag with everything she had found really useful— Imodium, Paracetomol and Germolene. At some point or other I was extremely grateful for each of these, particularly the latter while my backside was getting used to spending all day in the saddle. Other gifts included a tiny radio, a diary, a camping saucepan and a plastic document holder. Unfortunately none of these items came back with me; they were all broken or stolen at some point.

My next door neighbour had given me a bike some months earlier to make space in his garage and I cadged some saddlebags. The only things I actually bought were a good quality, lightweight sleeping bag and a water filter. This was a ceramic filter pump which weighed over a kilo and cost a hundred pounds but Joy had read about the nasty waterborne diseases you can get in Africa and she insisted I take it.

I had imagined it would come into its own in the Sahara but of course I never used it there, as there is no water. (Doh!) Where it really was a prized possession was in Sub-Saharan countries like Senegal, Mali and Burkina Faso where water is relatively freely available from village wells and pumps, but does need treating. It was only on the day I left home that I truly appreciated I would not be seeing my family again for a long time, and the realisation hit me hard. As I rode off I wondered, for the first but not the last time, whether this was something I really wanted to do. Fortunately, I had arranged to meet up with my friend Reg who had agreed to ride the first leg to Northern France with me. Just before midnight we pulled into the port at Folkestone to be told by a grizzled old gatekeeper, "There's not been a ferry from here these past eighteen months." The first of my many cock-ups. So we pushed on to Dover and eventually arrived in Calais at four in the morning.

We parted in Lille, as Reg had to get back to work, and I cycled alone through France, Spain and Morocco until I met another cyclist with whom I cycled through the Sahara. After that I spent a lot of my time with various cycling partners although by the time I got to Ghana I was alone again. From Accra, I took a flight, due east, over the trouble spots of Central Africa to Nairobi where I continued my journey down through East Africa. The final leg, from Durban to Cape Town, was with my younger brother, Steve, who said he wanted to share my adventure although I suspect he also wanted to keep an eye on his feebleminded sibling.

My book is partly about my journey, partly about the people I met and partly about my attempts to understand why the experience was such a disappointment.

I was disappointed on two levels. Firstly, I had set off thinking things in Africa were getting better: they're not, they're getting worse. Secondly, I was disappointed in travel itself. If I'm asked if I would recommend the experience to anyone else, the answer is no, not really. Would I do it again? Again, no. Do I think it was a worthwhile experience? No, definitely not. Oddly enough, Heinz had told me I would feel this way but I did not believe him.

Chapter 1

There is an old joke that white South Africans tell English tourists with evident relish. "What is the difference between an English tourist and a racist? Answer—about two weeks." They enjoy telling it because it makes them feel better about their own racism, less guilty because of the implication that inherently we all have the capacity to be racist, given the right circumstances. I heard it a couple of times at the end of my ride and, whilst I never found it very funny, I did come to appreciate its truth because, to my surprise and disappointment, I personally experienced the syndrome described in the joke.

I had set off with an unspoken but firm belief in the old adage about travel broadening the mind. I had never travelled as a "traveller" before—I had been a package tourist and I had been an independent holidaymaker. I had also travelled a bit on business. On this occasion, on my own with just a bicycle and a tent, and with a whole year in front of me, I thought I was joining that select band of hardcore travel junkies who turn their noses up at holidays and tourists. For them travel is a lifestyle, not just a break from routine. To occupy a place in the traveller hierarchy you must observe unspoken but strict rules—paid work is undertaken only to finance further travel and all forms of travel must be the cheapest and most basic available. The more uncomfortable the experience, the more "valid" it is.

You can tell when you are in the company of a hardcore traveller because they will tell you that everyone they met was really friendly. In reality, there is nowhere in the world where everyone is friendly, although there are definitely places where nobody is. For some reason these travellers either don't know this or don't accept it. Particularly difficult journeys are described with great relish—the overcrowded old bus which broke down in the desert for two days or the ferry trip which should have taken 48 hours and took a week. No food, no water, no sleep. It is a mistake to offer sympathy when you hear these stories as they will say, "Oh no, it was truly magical,—I shared a real experience with real people. I will never forget it."

I soon realised that I was never going to be accepted as a member of this exclusive club. I had not even packed in my job, only taken sabbatical leave. I was a part-time traveller, not much better than the truckloads of overlanders who are ten a penny in Africa. But at least I could look down on the tourists; everyone has more cred than they do.

I had decided to use a bicycle to get to South Africa, but for one reason or another, there were occasions when I had to use other means of transport. People look at me a bit oddly when I say this, but I found that a bike was the most comfortable and most stress-free way of getting around in Africa. In the normal course of events you can drink when you are thirsty, eat when you are hungry and sleep when you are tired. In the bush, I could relieve myself whenever necessary, more or less. These are comforts invariably denied to hardcore travellers in their "authentic" bush buses, ferries, trains, share trucks, or overloaded transit vans euphemistically referred to as "taxis." Compared with a bike, local transport is exhausting, unreliable and often bloody dangerous. People who looked upon me as a slightly deranged innocent didn't understand that my heart bled for every traveller's face that I saw jammed against the window of a battered old bus, goat on lap, water bottle long since empty. As these buses only start when they are full (which usually means more people than seats plus livestock) and are prone to breakdowns and other unscheduled and unexplained stops, it is impossible to estimate how long a trip will take. So you can never tell how long it will be before you get the chance to eat or drink and if you've got the runs you are in serious trouble. Just try asking a driver when he plans to stop for a toilet break and he will look at you as if you had asked when did he pass his driving test. No idea what you are talking about, but to make you happy he'll say, "Soon, soon," which in reality means you'll have a toilet stop the next time the engine conks out or a goat falls off the roof.

The worst part of my journey was a 13-hour train ride in Mauritania, which I had previously thought was a fictitious country like Ruritania, or perhaps a ship. I had ridden through the Western Sahara with a Japanese cyclist called Massami whom I had met en route. The first town over the border into Mauritania is Nouadhibou and from there the next target is Nouackshott, the capital, about halfway down the country, also on the coast. Unfortunately there is no road between these towns. It is possible to continue south by taking a four by four vehicle along the beach, while the tide is out, but you need a local guide or you will get lost or stuck. You also need a lot of food and water. I am told it is worth the effort, as the route takes you through one of the most spectacular bird sanctuaries in the world. However, it is not possible on a bicycle because the sand is often too deep, and, as there is no water en route, you simply could not carry all the water you need to take.

So Massami and I decided to take the train east into the desert to Choum, then follow a road shown as a little red line in the map southwest to an oasis town, Atar. From Atar there is a good tarmac road all the way to Nouackshott. We had met a bunch of hardcore travellers who also planned to use the train which was due to leave Nouadhibou at 3 p.m. the next day. This is no ordinary train. It transports iron ore from the mines in the heart of the Sahara to the port of Nouadhibou where it is loaded onto ships for export. It is officially both the longest and slowest train in the world. Although over two kilometres in length, it has only one passenger compartment. This is always so full that even hardened travellers get panic attacks, standing cheek by jowl like battery hens. For Massami and me, with our fully laden bikes and luggage, the passenger compartment was out of the question. We planned to travel with the couple of hundred other "passengers" who clamber onto the open ore wagons and jump off when they think they are where they should be. Nobody buys a ticket, nor is expected to.

When the train pulled in, the crowd waiting by the tracks surged forward to claim their places and Massami and I were lucky enough to find a flat truck onto which it was relatively easy to haul our bikes. Locals in flowing Arab dress with huge piles of baggage quickly occupied the space in the middle. Massami and I sat on the edge with the other European travellers, dangling our feet over the rails. The others consisted of a young Dutch couple—she was an artist who tried to sell me postcards of her paintings and he played traditional Dutch tunes on an accordion which was his pride and joy. He was unmistakeably Dutch with his Motorhead moustache and traditional cap. I had enjoyed his accordion playing the previous night, as I fell asleep in my tent, but I thought the post card paintings were pretentious rubbish. All stars and moons and dismembered body parts, particularly the ubiquitous "meaningful eye" that you always see in art of this type. With them was a big, serious German in search of the full travel experience. The last thing he wanted was for a bit of fun to get in the way and from what I saw, it rarely did. It had to be hard and it had to be "real." I never once saw him deign to speak to anybody except the accordion player, who quoted his thoughts to the rest of us with a totally unnecessary reverence. There was an easygoing New Zealander called Grant who had met an American girl, Leslie, in Morocco and they had become a couple, although the relationship was not to last much longer. I told her she shared her name with my dad but that he spelt it "Leslie." She told me she spelt her name the same way and was amazed that in England we had a male and female version.

Grant had enquired about buying a ticket for the passenger compartment—a major faux pas for a real traveller. Compartments are for tourists and Leslie spent almost the whole journey with her back to him.

TEN REASONS WHY AFRICA
WILL NEVER WIN THE WORLD CUP

As the train pulled out I reflected that things were starting to look up for me. I had been alone during the couple of months it had taken to ride across Europe and Morocco and at last I had managed to team up with another cyclist. Too bad that Massami planned to go only as far as Senegal where he intended to take a flight back to Europe. Too bad that he could hardly speak English, although I appreciated his company. Communication was slow and laborious but always well worth the effort.

Initially the late afternoon ride into the desert was pleasant; we chatted amongst ourselves and we had a bit of food and water, which was shared out. Even when the sun went down there was a huge new moon so that we could still see into the desert, although I must admit the unchanging scene was getting a bit monotonous. This part of the desert was a disappointment for me; not the rolling dunes that you see in French Foreign Legion films, more like a huge building site with rubble, sand and plastic bags blowing about. What turned it into a nightmare was after a couple of hours the train picked up speed and this threw up a cloud of iron ore dust. A silvery, choking powder with a strong pungent odour a bit like Ajax, it was soon in my hair and my nostrils and easily permeated my thin clothing. I envied the locals in their traditional robes and hoods who were completely protected against the stuff and seemed to be comfortably asleep in the middle of the truck. For me, falling asleep risked falling off the train.

Everyone knows that it gets very cold in the desert at night but thinking ahead has never been my strong suit and soon I was freezing. I borrowed a jacket from Leslie and wrapped my sleeping bag round my head and shoulders but still I was cold. As the train was so long any change in the engine speed caused a huge jolting in the rest of the train, like a Mexican wave. Each time, my backside would suddenly shoot six inches along the metal floor and this soon got very painful. I was very poorly prepared for a long train ride and I ran out of water and food. I was tired, fed up and uncomfortable and we still had about eight hours to go. For some reason, Grant decided to take a photo of me and I tried hard to smile in the harsh flashlight. Some weeks later he emailed the digital photo back to my family but they did not recognise the gaunt old man in his battered straw hat. Massami, who always thought ahead, gave me the occasional biscuit or sip of water but I did not want my carelessness to be too obvious and I tried to put on a show of reluctance before accepting. It was soon to become a feature of our relationship that Massami would bail me out with the necessities of life, usually food and water, but also with the odd spot of oil for my bike or plastic tie for something that had broken. He was never short of any item he might need.

Every two or three hours the train would stop somewhere in the middle of the desert. What a relief—you could stretch your legs and have a pee but you had to be quick because it would start again without warning. After all, it was not really a passenger train.

We stopped at about 5 a.m. and Massami told me this was Choum, our destination. It was just like anywhere else in the desert, with no buildings or sign, but I didn't care how he knew. I was just delighted to be free from the tyranny of the train. We got our bikes down and watched as the train disappeared farther into the desert. A truck pulled up alongside the track, offering rides to Atar, a hundred and twenty kilometres away. Grant, Leslie and the others clambered into the back and we promised to look for them when we got to Atar. Massami and I pushed our bikes fifty yards into the desert, put up our tents and slept like babies, albeit silver-coated babies.

When I woke up, I looked out the tent to see that Choum consisted of a group of shacks beside the railway lines. The little red line shown on my map was no more than a few tyre tracks heading south into the desert, hopefully to Atar. When we eventually got to Atar some days later and we met up with the others I was able to return Leslie's jacket. I asked her if that train ride wasn't the worst nightmare she had ever had? She seemed genuinely surprised and answered in true hardcore traveller style—"Oh no, I thought it was a wonderful, magical experience which I'll never forget." Silly me, of course it was.

The funny thing about the traveller hierarchy is that no matter where you position yourself, the locals see you as just another tourist. You can be dressed like a native, penniless and well off the tourist track, but to a local you are fabulously rich, a wallet on legs (or wheels in my case). There is no inhabited area in the world that is untouched by tourism and that means that people you meet see you as an opportunity to make money. They want to sell to you or guide you or beg from you or just cheat you. Most people who befriend you will eventually want to take you to their brother's carpet shop, or ask for money to pay for an education or to save a dying mother. However it is still possible to meet people who just want to talk, share views or simply to welcome you to their corner of the world. People with no desire to profit in some way from your appearance. I didn't come across many like this but there were some.

One day, in a remote part of Senegal, something odd caught my eye—a hammock slung between two trees by the side of the road. Hammocks are unusual in West Africa but what was even odder was that nobody had stolen it. It was just outside a prosperous-looking, walled villa. In this area most dwellings were simple mud huts surrounded by wattle fences. I couldn't resist trying out the hammock and after a hard morning in the saddle I began to doze. I was woken by a man shouting at me, his head just above the wall. Feeling a bit sheepish, I got ready to apologise for my cheek. The man came out the gate, led by two teenage boys. He was very handsome, about thirty-five and blind. He shook my hand, sat next to me and invited me to eat lunch with him. My philosophy was always to accept any offer of hospitality and his boys brought out the ubiquitous cheboujienne—the delicious national dish of oily rice and fish. We ate and talked and afterwards had tea.

He had been blinded about twelve years earlier by running into a branch of a tree. He also told me that he had left school at the age of 15 and that he had been a farmer. He had satellite TV and spent a lot of time "watching" European football. His French was much clearer and easier to understand than most Africans I met and I put this down to the TV. I never understood by what process he had become by far the richest man in the district, particularly as I don't think he was born into wealth. My French is not good enough to get to the heart of what was a pretty delicate question. But he did explain why he had a hammock outside his house—it was because it attracted people passing by. In all the years it had been there, nobody had ever tried to steal it and he had passed many hours in conversation with people from all over the world. It was his way of travelling.

But it wasn't just the gradual and rather disappointing realisation that I was usually regarded as a tourist with money rather than as an intrepid traveller that changed me from an English tourist to the racist of the South African joke. This was a process which commenced I know not where but which first came to my notice on a dusty road in Mali.

I had met a Dutch couple, Wim and Marlies, in Segou, a pleasant town in Mali with a panoramic view of the River Niger. They were on a ten-week cycling tour which had started in Bamako, the capital, and was to end at Accra in Ghana. We had a stroll around the town and watched the sun set over the river as the fishermen poled their flat-bottomed boats back to shore. The scene was beautiful but as so often in Africa the setting was ruined by one of those rubbish tips which just seem to spring spontaneously into existence. We discussed how Africans seemed not to care about rubbish, either as an eyesore or as a source of flies and disease. Previously I had been told by a hardcore traveller that African towns could not cope with the level of rubbish which was brought about by the growth of tourism. Looking at the piles of plastic bags, tyres and general refuse by the river at Segou, I rejected that argument. Firstly there weren't many tourists here and secondly it wasn't tourist rubbish. It was there because the river was close and it was the most convenient place to dump it. Crucially, it was there because the local Africans did not seem to mind that it was there.

I remembered staying at a beautiful beach campsite in Morocco where the owner cooked a delicious fish tajine and then just threw the vegetable peel and fish heads onto a rubbish dump in the middle of the otherwise perfect beach. He didn't seem to realise that this degraded his own campsite and made it less attractive to European travellers. He was a likeable, enthusiastic character but money mad and yet he didn't see the link between making money out of his site and keeping it clean and attractive. It was a similar story when Massami and I arrived in Nouackshott, having spent several days riding through the Sahara. We found a campsite on a beach but as I was putting up my tent my head was enveloped in a cloud of flies. It was midday, very hot and to be honest I was feeling a bit sick of Africa and all things African. I asked the owner where I could put some rubbish that we had brought with us out of the desert. He gestured vaguely and sure enough there was the open rubbish tip, just about in the middle of the site, swarming with flies.

A few weeks before, Massami and I had stayed at a campsite in Atar, shortly after the train ride from hell. The site was owned by Europeans and it was spotless. Rubbish was put into covered containers, which were regularly emptied, and the place was swept and tidied by a group of lads who seemed to know exactly what was expected of them. The toilets had doors with locks and the rudimentary showers worked well. It had taken us three days to get there from Choum and we were still caked in the silvery iron ore dust from the train. My first shower was one of the great pleasures of my trip. The Dutch lady who ran the place seemed to be a hard task master but she knew what people like us wanted in a campsite—and the comparative absence of flies was just bliss. The hard core travellers who had left us in a truck were staying in a locally run site half a mile away where the flies were horrendous. I once went there for a meal which we ate at a white plastic table. Every so often someone would bang the table to clear the hundreds of flies which settled amongst the food, but even then they were so brazen that not all of them would take to the air. I hated competing with flies for my food, particularly where force of numbers gave them the upper hand. Grant and Leslie used to come to our place where we had shade, chairs, free drinking water and clean toilets. Not quite as "real" but a darn sight more comfortable.

Marlies and Wim had also experienced lots of hotels and campsites and we agreed that in general, if they were European-run, they tended to be clean and well organised whereas African establishments were often dirty, disorganised and badly maintained. We discussed why this was so but we did not come up with a theory that satisfied us all.

The next day they took their bikes on a bus, as Marlies was having trouble with her knees and wanted a rest from cycling. A few days later I was being pushed by an immensely powerful wind into Mopti, an old city on a bend of the Niger, when I saw Marlies and Wim struggling against the gale as they tried to cycle to a town some fifty kilometres in the other direction. The wind was bad but much worse was the dust which had turned poor Marlies's eyes blood red. She looked exhausted and on the point of tears and I really did not envy them their journey but we said our hellos and goodbyes and I went into Mopti to find a campsite.

A few days after that I was in a cheap hotel in Bankass, just outside the Dogon Country which is a fascinating part of Mali and one of the few places I visited which really lived up to expectations. The hotel had been European owned and was described in my Lonely Planet guide as "smart." It was now in African hands and sure enough it had become run down. When I arrived at Reception the guy on duty had his feet on the desk and at no stage during the process of agreeing a price did he move from that position. Later, I was sitting in the grounds writing up my diary when the owner, Ali, joined me. I didn't particularly want company but Africans often don't seem to have the respect for other peoples' privacy that we stuffy Europeans find quite important. He was friendly and talkative. Having got from me that I had a daughter of marriageable age, he insisted that I take his rather unflattering photo home with me in the hope that I could persuade my daughter to come out and marry him. For a businessman and part owner of a hotel I was amazed he could be so naïve but what really struck me was that there were rooms in his hotel which he could not use because they were full of rubbish. Why not spend the two or three hours he had devoted to me and my daughter, clearing out a room and so make extra revenue? After all, the hotel was next door to an area which was probably the fastest growing tourist attraction in Mali and very handy for the coaches coming in from the airport in Ouagadougou. As tactfully as I could I asked Ali about this and as usual I could not elicit an answer that I could understand. He did not even stock Coca Cola and Fanta, the standard tourist drinks, and yet again I was left wondering why it was that a situation could be so under exploited, a feeling I experienced many times in Africa. He was sitting on a potential goldmine, success and opportunity beckoned, but he came to me for what he thought he wanted—my daughter's hand in marriage.

Having extracted a promise that I would speak highly of him to Adele, and so possibly become his father-in-law, Ali insisted that I take down my tent and sleep in a room, for free.

Under a huge fan, which kept the mosquitoes at bay, I slept soundly and in the morning was very happy to find that, by chance, Marlies and Wim had also ended up at this hotel. We all agreed to team up to ride to the next big city, Ougadougou.

As we cycled along the red dust roads Marlies made a comment which marked my first realisation that I was going through the "tourist to racist" syndrome. She said, "It isn't surprising, is it, that the early colonialists considered themselves to be so superior to the Africans?"

Initially I felt a bit disappointed that someone I liked as much as Marlies could make a comment like that, and I said that I thought Africans just were different and had a different outlook on life. It was their country and it wasn't our place to impose our irrelevant Western values on them. That was my stock response to any comment that I felt to be racist or superficial. But Marlies and Wim were certainly not racist and nor were they superficial. They greeted all the kids who waved at us and were happy to mix at any opportunity. They had genuine warmth for the local people whose exuberance excited them but often just irritated me. They both loved Africa and respected many aspects of African life. As I contemplated Marlies' words I began to see her point. The Africa I had seen so far was living up to its image— the people were friendly, curious and quick to see humour. They also appeared to be chronically disorganised and highly dependent on the white man's largesse. The women typically work very hard; they tend the fields, they raise the kids and they fetch the water and do the cooking. The men spend long hours sitting in the shade talking and usually come across as lazy and even a bit stupid.

I used to stop at little village shops to buy provisions like rice and onions and noticed that I often seemed to get the wrong change—not short changed, just wrong. It gradually dawned on me that African men were very poor at simple arithmetic, even when they had spent a lifetime running a shop or a small business. To be fair they were not just poor at it, they were absolutely hopeless and often seemed to just take a guess at even the simplest calculations. Wim would spend ages explaining how to add up two cokes and a Fanta but without much reward and we never really understood why it was so difficult.

As time went by I began to notice the weaknesses in Africans to which Marlies had referred, and I lost faith in their ability to run businesses, their villages and even their countries. It would irritate me that I could walk into a shop and then have to ask one of the guys hanging around outside if he was the owner and would he get off his arse and serve me. Their general lack of foresight drove me mad. Any transaction which involved getting a bit of change resulted in a lengthy wait as the seller searched the village for someone who could change a note worth just a bit more than what you had just bought. This even applied in city shops and hotels—getting change was always a hassle because nobody seemed to realise that to run a business you need to keep some change.

Without ever being able to put my finger on why, I came to accept the premise that was implicit in Marlies' comment even though I was not particularly happy with myself for doing so. However, it was only in Southern Africa, where I was threatened and attacked and truly scared that I became actually racist in my outlook.

It was ironic how the process of independent travel, which is supposed to broaden the mind, could have so narrowed mine. I had never considered myself a racist although I must admit I had never been subject to those pressures which can turn people into racists. When I was in Southern Africa I was a white man travelling alone on a bicycle and so was in a vulnerable situation. I didn't feel that I had the option of remaining neutral and I naturally took refuge in the "white" camp. It was only later, when I had taken stock of the whole experience, that the thought occurred to me that the experience had in fact broadened my mind in that I had had a taste of what it is like to be a racist. This is how it is for a lot of white South Africans: many of them don't want to be racist but fear and lack of contact opportunities make it very difficult to take the neutral road. I could not amble through the country, as I had through the rest of Africa, confident that I would be welcomed and supported by whites and blacks alike, so I tended to "side" with the whites and with the Asians who also seem to be in the white camp.

In Southern Africa I began to see blacks as a threat whereas in North and West Africa they had been a source of support. Previously, a village was a welcome sight—it was where I got my food or my water or just exchanged a bit of banter with the guys hanging around the local shop. In Southern Africa they call them "homesteads" or "townships" and these terms have a far more sinister connotation. They are places of danger and white cycle tourists are not welcomed as merely amusing distractions, good for a laugh and maybe a bit of business. The township is a place to get past as soon as possible and if you want a coffee or some food you go to the malls or smart cafes where the white people go, where it is "safe." It is one thing to become gradually critical of how black people live their lives and disparaging about their abilities, but it is only when you also become fearful that racism really takes a hold. I was constantly being told that what I was doing was dangerous to the point of stupidity. White people would stop me on country roads and insist that I put my bike in the back of their "bakkie" so they could take me to the next town and safety. Many could not believe that I could contemplate such a journey without carrying a gun. It was quickly pointed out that white people do not cycle alone and in fact the only time I saw white people on bikes in Southern Africa was when they were in organised groups with backup vehicles. Once, in a café in the north of South Africa, a guy on his way to Kokstadt said that he wanted to drive nearly 500 kilometres out of his way to take me to Cape Town—or else I was going to be killed and he did not want that on his conscience. I declined but each time I heard the warnings I got more nervous and eventually I came to feel like I was alone behind enemy lines. Groups of blacks in the distance became threatening and I had to get past them without making eye contact. Casual chats around where I came from and where was I going became a thing of the past. The process described in the old South African joke was beginning to take effect.

Chapter 2

The real turning point in my journey and in the process of becoming "racist" was the day I was arrested in Harare. Having been fairly isolated from the news for several months, I had not realised that Zimbabwe was in as bad a state as it was. Soon after entering the country I met a German couple who were cycling all over Africa and were heading for Victoria Falls. The guy told me that he had been in contact recently with his father who had told him that wherever he went in Africa he should not go to Zim because it was just too dangerous. There were serious foot shortages, crime was rife and worst of all, the government and its supporters hated whites, especially English whites. They were only there because they both had a passion to see Victoria Falls and they had decided not to tell his father that they were in Zimbabwe. I had already noticed a major difference in the country—everywhere else in Africa people along the road waved at me, shouted questions, offered to buy my bike. The kids laughed at me, chased me or went into dance routines. Sometimes all three. Here people just ignored me or gave me long hard stares. Instead of raucous shouts for sweets and money the kids would make a gesture I had not seen before—one hand on the belly while the other put invisible food into the mouth. These kids never smiled and were seriously hungry. Once, I noticed that a lorry had spilled a few ears of maize along the way and I felt a little better that at least there was enough food in the country to allow a little bit of waste. Then I turned the corner and came across a dozen women and children carefully picking up every grain. I decided that I would leave Zimbabwe by the shortest route and I also resolved not to tell my family that I had been in Zimbabwe until after I had got out.

As I approached Harare I pulled out the LP Guide to find a campsite and chose to stay at a backpackers' hostel near the centre in Hillside. It was cheap, offered camping as well as rooms and even boasted a swimming pool. I was lucky I chose this one, as I later discovered that the other ones mentioned had either closed down or been converted into brothels. Hillside is quite a smart suburb with large detached houses, lawns and plenty of trees. I had no idea who lived in the houses because they were all surrounded by huge walls and I never saw any residents. The only property in the area without a wall was the Hillside Backpackers. This was an old colonial house (the second oldest in Harare) which had been built by the grandfather of the middle-aged lady who ran the place. Sandy was a dispirited woman of English extraction who was watching her business and her life disintegrate before her eyes. As she watched she chain-smoked, drank and steadily got more and more depressed. There was only one other guest, a South African on his way north in a beaten-up Land Rover. He was stuck for a while, as he couldn't find diesel. The only good thing about cycling in Zimbabwe was that the roads were empty because there was so little fuel. Sandy told me that before Mugabe had gone mad she often had more than twenty-five people staying with her. These days she could go for months without any customers at all. There were hardly any tourists in the country which was not too surprising, as there was no way of getting about unless you had a bicycle.

I needed some currency and Sandy advised me to go not to a bank but to use a guy who ran the local internet café where you got about twice the official rate of exchange. Inflation is raging in Zimbabwe and the currency, like everything, is a mess. The largest note is worth about 20 pence so you need huge bundles to pay for any large items. When

I paid Sandy for my three days stay, I gave her bundles the size of breeze blocks. Too many notes to count, you just had to trust that each bundle was worth what it claimed to be.

When I first entered Zimbabwe I had intended to cycle south, take in the Zimbabwe Ruins and enter South Africa at Beitbridge. Now I just wanted to get to the closest border and leave as soon as possible. So I decided to head east back to Mozambique via the border town of Mutare. Having made my plans, I decided to do what I normally did in a major city—take advantage of having a bike to have a good look around. I wanted to see the city centre and in particular the cricket ground and the former Rhodesia House, now known as Zimbabwe House, home of Robert Mugabe. As I rode into the centre an old guy suddenly hurled himself from the pavement and seemed to be about to take a kick at me. Instinctively I pulled out into the centre of the road to avoid him and was amazed to see his boot flying inches from my head. It was a Kung Fu kick worthy of Eric Cantona but coming from a scrawny-looking sixty year old, I was impressed and disconcerted in equal measure.

There was hardly a white face to be seen on the city streets and to add to my general feeling of unease, it was the first day of a two day "stayaway," or general strike, called by the Movement for Democratic Change, the country's main opposition to Robert Mugabe's government. I had read in the only opposition newspaper, *The Daily News*, that mobs loyal to Mugabe were in the city to make sure that stores and businesses stayed open. I really admired the bravery of *The Daily News'* staff, as they were openly critical of the Mugabe regime, and I was surprised that they could get away with it. The paper has since been closed down and most of the staff are in jail. MDC supporters were being beaten up and there were constant exhortations on the government-sponsored radio for the people to ignore the stayaway and get to work "for the good of Zimbabwe." It was amazing that the articles that I read in the pro-government press were almost word for word what I heard on the radio—my first experience of a true police state.

There was a sudden commotion outside a supermarket and in my edgy state I thought the revolution had started. It turned out to be just another shoplifter getting collared but it added to the feeling that the whole town was getting ready to blow. I went to a chemist to buy a razor and was given a price about ten times higher than I would expect to pay in the UK, and was told it was because it had been imported. I decided to let my beard grow some more. In an effort to combat theft most shops asked you to show your receipt with your purchases before allowing you out. Prices were a joke—bottles of coke at the roadside cost 70 dollars, a few English pence, but a litre of juice (imported) was so expensive that even I could not justify buying it. For the locals all staple foods were prohibitively expensive and milk and bread were black market items. The only food that appeared to be freely available was maize which was grilled and sold at street stalls. The wonderfully varied street food which I had enjoyed all over North and West Africa was nowhere to be seen. Apart from my Kung Fu attacker everyone ignored me and I began to wonder why I had found the raucous greetings and questions earlier in my trip to be so irritating. It was a lot better than this quiet air of hostility.

I went to the cricket ground where there was no game but World Cup cricket was on a giant screen in the bar. Inside it was more like the old Salisbury—the only black faces belonged to the waiters and all that really mattered was cricket. Even though there was a guarded gate to enter the ground and guards at the door I was advised that my chained bike would not be safe outside and I was directed to bring it inside. I watched a bit of cricket, had a beer and enjoyed the feeling of not feeling threatened. Still nobody took any notice of me and I could not see any group who looked as though they might welcome the chance to talk to a lone English cyclist. This was very strange for me, as I had got used to attracting a bit of interest wherever I went. After an hour or so, and a very boring English pub lunch, I resolved to sneak a look at Zimbabwe House on my way back to my campsite. This was on an avenue which my LP Guide said was a curfew area between the hours of 6 p.m. and 6 a.m. Anyone in this area at this time could be shot without being asked questions. At midday it was just a busy, rather attractive tree-lined thoroughfare and although I didn't think

26

there was a problem, I asked a soldier on duty at the corner if it was OK for me to continue. He said it was and actually smiled and I rode along fairly confidently. I was disappointed that the house itself was not visible behind a high wall and at the end of the avenue I turned round to go back. As I passed the house for the second time a sentry motioned me over to him. My heart sank and suddenly I was scared. He asked me why I was cycling up and down the road. I explained that I was just a tourist having a look around the city (which was very beautiful just like the country etc etc). He insisted I had been cycling up and down the road all morning. I said no, I had just come from the cricket ground. Another soldier, with insignia on his shoulders, joined us and belligerently asked me to explain what I was doing there. I was only halfway through my story when another soldier, also quite senior, butted in to demand to know what was I doing. I started again but he told me to empty my rucksack onto the floor. This guy had the meanest face I have ever seen, heavily pockmarked skin tightly drawn over his skull. The only soldier whose face I can still see clearly today. I could see that he really hated me and I just hoped that this guy would not be the one who would decide what was to happen to me. He said that I was a spy for Tony Blair and that my travellers' cheques were to be used to pay the agitators of the MDC. I had forgotten about the stayaway and kicked myself for my stupidity in thinking that I could do the site seeing tourist bit at such a tense time. Other soldiers came and went and I retold my story several times, with questions constantly being fired at me. "Why does Tony Blair want to bomb Iraq? Why does he hate Zimbabwe?" Explaining that Tony Blair had been a big disappointment to me too didn't seem to help.

After an hour the mean one told me to put my belongings back into my bag and get my bike. He took me back to the road and I was feeling intensely relieved that he seemed to be letting me go. I told him how wonderful his country was and that I totally agreed that Tony Blair was a madman. I could have cried when he took me to another gate and told me I was going to be detained. I was very aware that the area became a shoot-to-kill zone in a few hours. Inside the gates was a compound with a small wooden building and about fifteen or twenty soldiers lounging about. They gathered round me and started shouting at me and yet again I started explaining why I was there, that I was cycling through Africa for a charity and that I was not a spy. Some were very young and some were laughing; others seemed to be angry. One put his rifle barrel right into my face and said today was the day I was going to die. Somebody else pressed a revolver against my cheek and said he would shoot me at six o'clock. He said nobody knew where I was and that to shoot me would not be a problem. All the time I was trying to stay calm and to give the impression that I knew they were only joking, but when I was told to hand over my papers my hand was shaking violently, and this caused a fair amount of merriment. A very fat man who appeared to be in overall command turned up. He was the only one not in uniform but all the others appeared to show deference. I knew I was in real trouble when he put his face an inch from my face and bellowed at me. He stank of whisky and I realised that he was very drunk, so drunk that he was incoherent. Great gobs of spit kept landing on my face but I didn't dare wipe it off.

By this time the contents of my bag were again on the floor, and army boots were kicking around my possessions and my multi tool kit was in bits and considered to be, with my travellers cheques, further proof that I was a spy.

As the hours went by, and the closer we got to six o'clock, the more terrified I became. There was no point where someone was not shouting at me or threatening me and I was told repeatedly that I would be shot at six. Occasionally they broke off into another language and I thought they were arguing about who would shoot me. I had stopped trying to act cool and just stood there quietly waiting, kicking myself for my stupidity and my arrogance. I remembered my wife had said to me before I left the UK that she thought she would never see me again, that I would be killed and my body left unfound in the bush. I thought, *My God she was right.* I felt tempted to break down in tears, get down on my knees and beg for forgiveness. If I'd have thought that would have helped I'd have done it.

A few minutes before six, an army Land Rover was driven into the compound and the mean one told me to get into the back, with my bike and my belongings. I don't know why, but I asked him where was he going to take me. I was conscious that I sounded pathetic and that my lip was quivering. He said that they were going to "teach me a lesson." One of the younger soldiers put his rifle to his shoulder as if in answer to my question. I had long since ceased attempting to smile at gestures like this. I got in the back where the metal grill made me think of all the other poor sods who had been transported in this vehicle. I still felt in my heart of hearts that it was unlikely they would actually shoot me; strange how being a British subject still seems to confer a sense of inviolability. Nonetheless I was pretty sure that I was going to get a beating. I had not seen either the driver or his companion before and they were both in civilian dress. I tried to strike up some form of conversation but was ignored. For the first time in Africa, I really wanted the opportunity to resolve a situation with the traditional bribe, but fortunately decided against making the first move.

As we slowly drove off I noticed that the sky had darkened and to add to the tension I could hear the odd clap of thunder. At least the mean bastard wasn't with us. We drove very slowly, only about 15 mph, and stopped after ten minutes at a street corner where the driver spoke to a group of people whom I took to be undercover agents watching who was doing what during the stayaway. This was repeated several times and I noticed that more and more people were coming onto the streets and mobs were beginning to form. Occasionally during the street corner conversations the driver would jab his thumb at me as if in some kind of explanation. After about an hour I could not resist asking again where they were taking me and the driver said I was to be detained by the CIO. Even I had heard of the feared Central Intelligence Office, as these were the people who dragged opposition activists out of their beds to kill and beat them. I asked him why and he said because I was a spy. We drove to Harare Central Police Station which is an impressive building with a bank of broad steps and stone pillars, just in front of the bus station where a large mob had formed. With my rucksack on my back, I carried my bike up the steps and into the reception of the building where I was handed over to the CIO.

A CIO guy, with a strangely respectful air, led me down a corridor to an office with several plain-clothes men sitting on a bench which went round three of the walls. Against the other wall was a table with a typewriter and a lot of untidy paperwork. From time to time the men got up and left and eventually only the officer to whom I had been handed over remained. He was quite young and seemed eager to please his boss who had told him to get my details. He asked me to explain what I was doing in Harare and when I had finished he asked me to write it all down. I was feeling a lot more secure with the CIO than I had felt with the Army because nobody was drunk, or even threatening, and for the first time my details were being committed to paper. For some reason this made me feel a lot more confident—at least there was some evidence that I had actually been here. He knew that I had a diary and asked me for it. This was taken away and for the next couple of hours I was on my own. I went through the contents of my rucksack and was quite surprised to see that all of my possessions seemed to be still there. I used to write in my diary every day and usually at some length—not just about where I had been but also about my impressions and some of the conversations I had. They must have read it very carefully because every so often an officer would ask me to explain what I meant by a certain phrase or to clear up some ambiguity caused by my poor handwriting. I had never re-read it and was desperately trying to remember what I had written, particularly about Zimbabwe. I was sure that I had never mentioned Robert Mugabe and was grateful for that.

Outside I could hear the thunder and occasional crowd noises, reminiscent of the distant mob you hear off stage in a play. African cities are all dangerous at night but tonight Harare was definitely no-go for a lone Englishman. I was almost glad to be inside and assumed that I would be held at least for the night. I kept asking for permission to call Sandy at the campsite, as she would be worrying where I was. Maybe she was and maybe she wasn't but at least they knew that someone else knew I was in Harare. I was still scared but more confident than at any time since being arrested.

At about ten the young officer came in, gave me my diary and told me I could go. Suddenly I thought of the rampaging mobs outside and I almost asked if I could stay in a cell overnight. My senses came to me just in time—get out while the going's good—and I wheeled my bike back along the corridor. Bizarrely, the CIO man was telling me that he had always wanted to visit England and I told him if he did he must come and stay with me; after all, he had my address.

Outside, at the top of the steps, he shook my hand but as I carried my bike down I saw a group of people charging towards me from the far side of the bus station. Frantically I jumped on my bike and pedalled in the other direction, half expecting a hand to grab me from behind. At each corner I stopped to see if the coast was clear, and if I was seen I was chased. I was in enemy territory and once again I felt the terror rising in me. It was dark and thundery and whilst I could hear mobs I didn't know where they were and so knew that I could be engulfed at any moment. My legs were shaking even as I pedalled. Although I was zigzagging all over the city, I suddenly recognised a road which I knew would take me back to the campsite and in 15 minutes I was back. Nobody was about and the house was in darkness. As I crawled into my tent I bitterly regretted the fact that this was the only property in the area which was not protected by a high wall. The CIO knew where I was and could come back for me at any time. Or worse still, the army. I resolved to leave the next day and as I got down into my sleeping bag I was still shaking with fear.

During the night I was wakened by fire crackers which I assumed were connected with the mobs in the city. The second and third time that I heard them I realised it was actually gunfire but by then I was almost past being scared.

The next morning I told Sandy what had happened to me and I remember feeling a tinge of disappointment that she didn't seem to feel it was any big deal. She had been living with it a long time, she wasn't just passing through like me. Even so, she said I had been extremely lucky not to have been shot or beaten up, and in fact I read in *The Daily News* that two men had been beaten to death that night, one in the same cells in which I had been held. Clearly my diary had revealed that I was just a naïve tourist on a bicycle after all and not

Tony Blair's spy, but I still don't understand why the soldiers did me no physical harm when it would have been so easy—and they so obviously wanted to. Much later on, in Mozambique, I was robbed while I slept and at first I was distraught that I had lost my passport and travellers cheques. Later on I realised that I had actually lost something that was far more valuable to me, and had probably saved my bacon that day—my diary.

Whilst I had been nervous before, largely because of the dire warnings I was getting from local whites, from that day on I developed an innate fear which never really left me. I found comfort and security in white surroundings and felt vulnerable on the road or when I was alone. Apart from those blacks who I met in the conventional circumstances, that is serving whites in some way or other, I never spoke to blacks and quickly lapsed into stereotyping them in the fashion of the local whites. I always felt a frisson of fear when I saw armed black soldiers or police. In fact I was becoming, in both attitude and behaviour, just like the typical racist South African so vilified by decent liberal-minded Englishmen. I felt disappointed and even a bit guilty to find that I felt like this and wondered whose fault it was. Was it mine because I had failed to understand and to empathise with the difficulties experienced by African blacks? Was it colonialism, globalisation or corporate Western exploitation that left them weak and dependent? Or was it their fault because they are disorganised, undisciplined, superstitious, corrupt and violent?

If travel had broadened my mind in any way it was to give me some empathy with a group of people I had previously despised for their racism. I had experienced the fear that many whites have for blacks and I responded in the time-honoured way—stay away from the "black" areas and as far as possible, live, work and play with other whites. This is easy in South Africa because it is still the way the different races live, and to buck this system is to invite ridicule and hostility from both sides. Apartheid is officially dead in South Africa but apartness is still kept alive by the twin pillars of racism—fear and ignorance. Since getting back to the UK I have lost much of the intensity of the racist feelings I had in Southern Africa, but I will never forget what it felt like to have had them.

Chapter 3

Is it too obvious to be worth mentioning that a journey is shaped more by the people you encounter than the places you visit? Before I set off I mused that my experience would be affected dramatically by when I left, because if I left say a week or even a day early I would meet a totally different set of people. You can cross the Sahara and see the same desert but the people you meet en route will determine the experience more than anything else. The ancient Chinese had a proverb that describes this perfectly—"The same man cannot enter the same river twice—it is not the same man and it is not the same river."

I was lucky enough to meet Massami and spend a couple of months with him in Mauritania and Senegal. If I had left England a week later I might not have met him and so might have crossed the desert with someone else or (God help me) on my own. When I reflect on my journey and on my experiences, it is always in the context of the people who were around at the time. The scenery, the weather, the food, all of these things have an impact on your experience but nothing determines the nature of your experience like the people you encounter. A journey made alone will be totally different from a journey made with a companion. Different companions result in different experiences. A journey will be forever coloured by whether the man in the street steals your wallet or offers you his friendship. Which one you meet is down to when you are there, and that is determined by when you started the journey. Perhaps it is too obvious to be worth mentioning.

By the time I got to Northern Spain I had been cycling for over a month but I had not met anyone that really stood out in my memory until I met Mac. I had arrived at a deserted campsite (this was October, after all) just south of Salou where two children were meticulously sweeping up the leaves and debris in the well-maintained camping area. They were clearly brother and sister and I learned that they were Rumanians whom the site owner had taken in, and was helping to get them residency in Spain. In the meantime they seemed happy to work as hard and as cheerfully as anyone I came across in my entire trip. I asked the girl if I could stay and she indicated that she had to telephone the owner to establish the price. Eventually she came back to say it was ten euros a night and I put up my tent and went to take a much-needed shower.

In the shower block a huge Scotsman in his sixties asked me how much I had paid to camp. He told me he was paying 3 euros a night because he had come to an arrangement with the owner whereby each week he stayed was cheaper than the preceding week. He had been there over a month. As he dried himself off he told me which was the best shower to use and invited me round to his tent that evening for drinks. I had not had much contact with anyone for a while and was pleased to accept, particularly as I never refused hospitality. He was right about the shower but with hindsight I should have been warned by the obvious pleasure he got from describing every detail of the deal he had secured with the owner.

I strolled over to Mac's tent, which he had rigged in such a way that he had his own little courtyard in the corner of the campsite. He told me he had arranged things so that he could sit by his tent unobserved but he could see anyone who approached. Sensible in a war torn jungle but, hey, this was the Costa Brava. He was genuinely pleased to see me and he poured me a drink of brandy and honey. It was quite nice, even though the honey came from one of those little pots you get free at breakfast on cross channel ferries. I remarked that after two months with only a plastic cup, it was great to drink out of a glass. That was about all I said, or was able to say, for the rest of the evening. Clearly Mac was a very lonely man and he latched onto this opportunity to pour out his life story to me. He told me that he had spent the previous evening "in conversation" with a German called Helmut until two o'clock in the morning. My heart bled for poor Helmut who clearly lacked the language skills or the bravura to get away before then. I have met, and been bored by, people who think conversation is a one-way process but Mac was in a class of his own. He apologised constantly for hogging the conversation but still did not give me a chance to say anything, and when I did he ignored me. I tried to get drunk but remained stubbornly sober. Making a break for it was impossible, as I was literally unable to squeeze in a, "Well I've been riding all day, better go to bed." I felt even more sympathy for the hapless German, and just hoped he had managed to get plastered.

Mac was a sad and bitter man who had been shafted by life—his wife had left him, he had lost his job, his friends had betrayed him. He had taken his employers to an industrial tribunal and although right was on his side, he had still lost the case. This was because the judge was inadequate and nothing to do with the fact that he had spurned the offer of legal assistance in order to represent himself.

He was in the area looking to buy a retirement property but the prices were far too high, a joke. He hated the Spanish but was especially vitriolic about the ex-pat Brits who ripped him off in their overpriced bars and the elderly English ladies who agreed to dates and then failed to turn up. He had advertised for "a lady companion" to accompany him on his trip and had met three candidates before he set off. Unfortunately none of them really measured up and so missed out on four weeks in a tent with Mac and his Ford Escort Estate.

The next morning I packed up my bike and decided to say goodbye to Mac from the saddle to avoid getting snared again, but he called me over and gave me a parcel. Later that day I opened it to find a little pot of P & O honey and the glass that I had admired the previous night. It had all been carefully wrapped in an unused bandage. Mac was at heart a generous and kind man and to this day I feel guilty for sneering at him. I just hope he can learn to hide his desperation, play down his desire to impress, and then maybe find the affection he craves. In the meantime, if ever I meet him again, I'll make sure I give him a very wide berth.

There were other people who I came across, some only fleetingly, but in their own way they all left a lasting impression and coloured my view of that part of the world. For example, Layoune to me will always be about three characters I met during the thirty-six hours I spent there.

Layoune is a military town dominated by the presence of the United Nations. Most of the vehicles you see are huge four by fours with "UN" plastered on the side. It is on the Moroccan coast and whilst it is not quite in the Sahara, it is hot, dry and sandy. Arriving in early December, I decided to buy some presents for my family, take them to a post office and send them off in time for Christmas.

Just off the spectacular main square there was a row of silversmiths, and as all three of my family like silver, it looked like all my shopping could be done at one stop. It felt very important to buy something they would like and, as it was late, I decided to come back the next day to peruse the items at leisure. The only campsite was twenty-four kilometres to the south, but being a UN town, the hotels were far too expensive so I set off, knowing that I would have to retrace my steps the following day.

As I got to the outskirts of the city, by a huge rubbish dump in the sand, two scavenging dogs on the horizon looked up and gave chase. Although they were some distance away, they were big and fast and despite my desperate pedalling, they were gaining on me. A man at the roadside saw my predicament and picked up a rock. At this the dogs pulled up and turned away. Dogs in Morocco are hated and feared and they all recognise the action of a man picking up a stone. The man shouted at me to stop, presumably to pay him for his trouble, but I was not for stopping anywhere near those dogs. A second later the rock came whistling past my right ear.

Being saved and then nearly decapitated by the same man within the space of ten seconds gave me plenty to think about as I rode the remaining twenty kilometres. By the time I got to the site, I had formulated a new rule which I adhered to throughout my journey in Africa. I would offer to pay for any service rendered to me. No more free lunches.

The site was deserted and in any case was full of brand new chalets; it was no longer a camp site at all. Nonetheless, the lad in charge, Ahmed, told me I could put up my tent on a paved area (the interior of my tent could be erected without pegs) and he charged me a nominal fee. There was no toilet block but he gave me the key for a luxurious chalet which he invited me to use as I wished. The site was on the edge of a purpose built holiday resort with a fantastic beach but no open shops and no restaurants. I watched the sun go down and braced myself for another hungry night. Ahmed came to me and asked if I would like to join him and his brother for a fish tajine. He told me to be ready at ten, way past my normal bedtime, but I was only too happy to wait up. At ten o'clock he set a table outside "my" chalet and I was given a magnificent tajine and a huge plate of fresh grilled fish. I was a little disappointed to be eating alone, as I had expected Ahmed and his brother to join me, but they had already eaten. I ate every scrap and asked Ahmed to tell me what I owed. He said that he had caught all the fish himself, he had enjoyed preparing it and that there was no charge. He wouldn't even let me wash the dishes.

In the morning I offered Ahmed my cycling sunglasses, one of my prized possessions, but all he would take was the tiny fee we had previously agreed for camping. As I cycled back to Layoune, past the dog attack rubbish dump, I kept a look out for my saviour so that I could belatedly settle up with him, but he was nowhere to be seen. Nor were the dogs although I had rocks in my pockets, just in case.

At the row of silversmiths, I studied the wares in the windows and came to the conclusion that they all sold much the same kind of stuff. The owners of each shop begged me to come in and I knew that I would have to go through the extensive bargaining process, so beloved by Moroccan traders, and I decided to get all my gifts from one shop.

At home I am a pretty uncommitted sort of shopper but on this day I was determined to get exactly what I wanted: I wasn't after tokens. Eventually I settled on a shop whose owner spoke good English and looked reasonably honest. He told me his name was Mohammed. I told him that I wanted three gifts, one for my son, one for my daughter and one for my wife. We agreed that I should choose the items and we would agree on a price afterwards. For an hour we pored over his goods and I chose jewellery for my wife and daughter and a silver knife in a sheath for my son. The price negotiations took another twenty minutes or so and eventually we arrived at a sum which seemed fair for us both. I told him that before I finally agreed to the transaction, I wanted to walk round the square and think of each member of my family in relation to their gift just so that I was completely happy with my choice. This would take me about ten minutes and I asked him to put the items to one side until I came back. Aghast, he moved to the door to block my exit. If I wanted a lower price we could talk more. I explained that this was not part of my bargaining tactics and that I really wanted just to consider the items, not the price. Within the next few moments he had brought the price down to about half what we had agreed. He brought out of his pocket an empty cigarette packet and claimed that the reason he was so keen to sell was that he was desperate for a smoke but had no money. Starting to smell a rat, I began to move out and as I physically moved him aside, the price came down to about a tenth. With a feeling of intense disappointment, I realised that my gifts were junk and I walked away. In my imagination, I saw Mohammed gazing sadly at his empty cigarette pack, to the strains of the old "Happiness is a cigar called Hamlet" advert, and this cheered me a bit.

I still had to go to the post office, as my camera was not working (the film was stuck inside), and I wanted to send it back to the UK so that I didn't lose any pictures. Still feeling very let down, I found the office and walked into a seething mass of people in a hall where eventually I was able to explain what I wanted. I was directed to an adjoining office where, in equally chaotic circumstances, I had to fill in a form and was then given a flat piece of cardboard which I had to manipulate to create a box. With the help of half a dozen excited customers, I ended up with a structure like a shoebox and then had to go back next door for some stamps. The whole process took well over an hour and I was more irritated than interested by the experience, although I was pleased that I had managed to send my camera back to England. A month later my family was mystified by the arrival of a box covered in Moroccan stamps, containing nothing other than an official export form. I never saw the camera again.

In their own ways Ahmed, the Dog Man and the shop owner all added to my experience of Layoune and each one prepared me a little better for Africa. I learnt something from each of them, but on a different day, different people would have given me a different impression but perhaps a similar lesson.

Chapter 4

I learned of Massami's existence long before I met him because drivers in the Western Sahara used to stop and tell me there was a Japanese cyclist about three hundred kilometres behind me. Very often these drivers were taking old Peugeots and BMWs from Europe to sell in Senegal—it wasn't that lucrative but it paid for the trip and for the next car. I felt pretty confident we would meet sooner or later as surely he was faster than me and there is only one road through the desert. Sure enough, as I was resting at the side of the road with a French couple, Phillippe and Francine, in a battered dormobile, he appeared on the horizon. I couldn't contain my excitement as we waited for him and for the first half hour he could do nothing but giggle and bow. Francine gave him a coffee and one of her fantastic little cakes and I asked him if he would mind if I could ride with him. His English was so poor that I could not work out if it was ok with him or not, but he seemed happy enough and I vowed to stick with him anyway. Phillippe and Francine were stuck in sand and had spent the previous night (their first wedding anniversary) in this spot, where I had chanced upon them. We waited with them until an Italian couple in a huge four by four turned up to pull them free. They were quite unconcerned about being stuck—they got stuck from time to time but knew that somebody would be along to give them a hand. Their happy-go-lucky approach contrasted sharply with the attitudes of most of the drivers I met in the desert, who made meticulous plans and were prepared for every possible eventuality. Back home in France they followed fairs around selling Phillippe's craft work and Francine's delicious little homemade cakes. I had no doubt about which was the more profitable, and said so, but Francine graciously insisted it was her husband's art.

The first thing that struck me about Massami was his appearance. Being Japanese he naturally stood out in the Sahara, but he was also dressed head to toe in exotic cycle racing gear. I wore a tee shirt, a sun hat and shorts, just like all the other travellers. Massami was in full body lycra with spuds and racing helmet. He could have stepped out of the peloton of the Tour de France. He gave the impression that he was fairly short but after he had finally stopped bowing I realised he was taller than I thought.

There is a strange ritual that cyclists go through when they meet each other—they lift each other's bikes to see how heavy they are. Dogs sniff each other and cyclists lift bikes. In Massami's case, though, I literally could not raise his bike off the ground. It must have weighed well over fifty kilograms, about twice the weight of mine, which was heavy enough. His bike was a state of the art beauty and probably very light but he just carried so much heavy stuff. As I got to know him I began to understand why Massami's bike was so heavy. He was a chef in a Japanese restaurant in Dusseldorf and he loved cooking. I will never forget the first meal he prepared. It was after the hellish train ride to Choum.

We had woken up by the railway tracks, took a compass reading and headed south into the desert. As we passed the clump of shacks that was Choum we were accosted by a ragged man with a maniacal stare who started shouting at us to come and stay at his hotel, although which shack was his "hotel" was not immediately obvious. The more we declined his invitation, the more furious he became. He obviously didn't get too much passing trade and was very indignant that he was missing out on what little there was. I had assumed that we would stock up with food and water before heading out but this guy was getting so angry that I was happy to follow Massami's lead and clear out as soon as possible.

For some reason, probably the euphoria of meeting up with another cyclist, I had completely misjudged the scope of the ride from Choum to the next target town which was Atar. On my map there was a little red road which I took to be tarmac. In fact it wasn't even a dirt road but a series of wheeltracks in the sand which sometimes came together but often were so far apart that it was easy to lose them altogether. I also had guessed it was about forty kilometres and so was thinking in terms of about half a day's ride. The fact that I had about half a day's food and water therefore did not disconcert me unduly.

After about four hours in the baking sun we had covered about fifteen kilometres according to Massami's cycle computer, most of it pushing or dragging the bikes through the sand. I got quite a shock when Massami showed me his map which indicated that the total distance to Atar was a hundred and twenty kilometres. There were no villages or habitation en route and at no point was there a tarmac stretch. We had not seen any other person since leaving Choum and I began to get a bit nervous, especially when Massami said we were probably on the wrong track. We knew we were heading in the right direction, due south, but we needed to get onto the track which was used by the trucks and four by fours. In the distance, to the west, we could see a line of boulders which looked like they could be the edge of a more formal kind of track and we decided to drag our bikes through the deep sand to get there. About an hour later we got to the stones but had invested a lot of our energy and water in doing so. When he saw that the stones were just a random formation in the desert, Massami started laughing uncontrollably. Slowly it dawned on me that I was lost in the desert with little food, even less water and that my longed-for companion was a total nutter.

My mind went back to my meeting with Heinz Sturke and his warning that twenty-fours in the desert without water usually spelt certain death. For the first time on my trip I felt that I was in real danger and, after he had calmed down a bit, Massami calculated that we had just enough water to last until the following morning. I was bitterly disappointed in myself and my apparent inability to plan ahead. Coming through Morocco I had experienced a couple of hungry nights and sometimes a few thirsty ones but here, in the middle of the desert, my lack of foresight was getting life threatening.

We struggled back towards the original track, still heading south. The ground got more rocky and we were able to ride rather than push our bikes. We saw two very young children with water carriers and hurried over to them to ask where the water was. They were the first people we had seen since the Sahara's version of Basil Fawlty. Unsurprisingly, they took fright and ran off. We followed them and came upon a huge white tent with a small knot of people staring at us in amazement. There was a man of about forty who I took to be the head of the household, three adult women, a handful of toddlers and a baby. In broken French I explained that we were trying to get to Atar. His jaw dropped even farther and he gestured questioningly at the bikes. I said yes, on these bicycles. His head started shaking slowly. He asked if we wanted water and as casually as I could I said that would be very nice. A young girl appeared with a leather gourd holding about 5 litres of water and started filling the various water bottles which Massami and I were carrying. Half-heartedly I tried to protest that we didn't want to take all their water but the man insisted that we fill our bottles. My mother had given me some nice little trinkets to take with me as gifts and I produced the best of these to give each of the women a brooch or necklace. They were delighted and put them on and chattered excitedly. The man was obviously pleased to see his womenfolk so happy and he invited us into the tent for tea. I was a little surprised to see Massami demur but I was already on my way inside and he followed. The ladies prepared the tea in traditional style, mixing in the mint and sugar and pouring from a great height to form a froth. Apparently this is done in the desert so that any dust in the air settles on the froth and not in the tea. I love this tea, in the desert it is just the best drink on earth. A child walked in with a huge plate of steaming rice and my cup of happiness overflowed. The plate was set down before the three of us and our host invited us to dig in. Having slaked my thirst I was very hungry and needed no second invitation,

I didn't even feel embarrassed that the women and children seemed to be waiting for us to finish. One of the girls noticed that I was struggling with my fingers, although Massami was doing fine. This caused general amusement but she gave me a large spoon and my rate of consumption doubled. I normally feel a little inhibited when eating from a communal plate, and in front of an audience, but on this occasion I had no such compunction and it was as well that it was such a large plate. As a vegetarian I should have put aside the tiny pieces of goat or camel that were mixed in with the rice but with about a hundred kilometres still to go, all I put aside were my principles.

After we had eaten we waited for the second sitting of women and children to finish and then we offered to pay for our meal. This was refused but we insisted and the family accompanied us outside where the man pointed out the right track to follow. This was a lot better defined than the track we had been on and with full water bottles and full bellies we set off feeling a lot more confident than we had been two hours earlier.

An hour later we saw the first vehicle of the day and that made us feel even better. The track was firmer and we had to push our bikes only occasionally through the sand. Late in the afternoon, having covered a good forty kilometres, I flagged down a truck (they were passing at the rate of about one an hour) and asked to buy some water. The driver sold us enough to refill our bottles and also threw in a couple of loaves of bread. I assumed that our evening meal would be bread and water and I was delighted at the prospect, it was such an improvement on our situation earlier in the day. Impossibly things got even better. As I was putting up my tent I noticed that Massami was setting up a gas stove and from somewhere deep in his saddle bags he produced little bottles of seasoning, soy sauce, a tin of tomatoes, a packet of spaghetti and even a carton of Parmesan cheese. No wonder his bike was so heavy. The meal was just superb, under a full moon with Massami's radio playing Arabic music in the background. No flies and no mosquitoes. To cap it all, Massami carried a portable seat which he insisted I sit on while he sat cross legged on the sand. Still covered in the pungent iron ore dust from the train, I reflected on how well things had turned out when my lack of planning could so easily have led to disaster.

The rest of the journey to Atar was relatively uneventful. We sheltered from the sun during the hottest hours each afternoon and cadged water and bread from passing trucks. A couple of days later we climbed a steep incline and at the top we could see palm trees and the oasis town of Atar. From here the road was tarmac all the way to Nouackshott.

In the clean and well-run campsite we showered, rested and met up again with our friends from the train journey. They were surprised to see us so soon and had taken bets on whether Massami and I would make it, as they had seen that the track was very sandy—in the opinion of some, too sandy to cycle. Like me, they had anticipated a relatively easy journey from the train to Atar but, if anything, they had a harder time than we did. When they boarded they thought they were going to have the back of the truck to themselves and that they would go straight to Atar. It doesn't work like that in Africa. The truck went to another stop to wait for more passengers. By dawn it was so crammed with people, livestock and luggage that they were left clinging to the frame of the truck, as it trundled for over ten hours through the desert. They had only one stop and this was for Muslim prayers. For all that Massami and I had been through, I would not have been willing to swap our bikes for their truck.

The campsite was the perfect place for me and Massami to rest up for a few days. It was very clean, had a central shaded area with chairs and books and even free, filtered water in a large cool vat. We played cards, (Grant's version of Gin Rummy), drank water and Massami serviced both his bike and mine. He had all the tools, another reason why his bike was so heavy. He loved working on bikes and was almost as good a mechanic as he was a chef—the perfect cycling partner. After he had finished, my bike ran like new. The next day, a Belgian guy on a motor bike whom I had met in Morocco turned up and we had another recruit for the Gin Rummy sessions. Luc was a gifted card player and was able to understand Grant's very complicated (and very flexible) rules. At long last, someone other than Grant began to win a few hands.

The whole group decided to visit the ancient Islamic city of Chinguetti which was only a few hours truck ride away. The Dutch couple and the dour German negotiated a deal with the owner of a pickup truck on our behalf. They enjoyed bartering with the locals and invariably secured a reasonable deal although no doubt even they had to pay the foreigners' premium. At this point Grant and Leslie were still a couple although things had obviously got a little tense since Grant's unfortunate attempt to buy a ticket for the train, which had so damaged his traveller cred. During a discussion on all-time favourite songs, Grant claimed the first record he had ever bought was *Ticket to Ride* by the Beatles, which I thought was pretty ironic.

We settled ourselves into the back of the pickup but before we had gone a mile, we pulled into a scrap-yard and a huge, greasy Massey Ferguson engine was loaded into the back. We were left perched on the tailgate, trying not to appear too perturbed by the driver's efforts to dislodge us over the bumps. I wondered if maybe our fellow travellers had negotiated just a bit too hard.

When we got there the group split into two as we set off round the old city. Grant came with me, Luc and Massami and Leslie went off with the Dutch couple and the German. The city is fascinating and is one of the holiest places in the Islamic world, even though long ago it lost its role as a major stopover on the old salt route through the Sahara. It is also getting covered by sand as the desert encroaches more each year. The French have built an airport nearby and there are direct flights from France three days a week so you have to be careful when you visit or you have to jostle with hundreds of French tourists. Where there are tourists there is a tourist trade and the street traders at Chinguetti were as persistent as any in Africa, ruining any chance of a quiet stroll around the city. Grant made the mistake of admiring a large wooden statue and the trader followed him for over an hour, even though he explained that he was a backpacker and could not cart such a heavy object with him. The would-be seller said that was no problem—he would put it in a bag for him! There was always an answer to every objection.

The agreement with the truck driver was that he would turn up at four p.m. to take us back to Atar. As expected he tried to claim that we had only paid for a one-way trip and that we had to pay more for the return. We ignored this and climbed into the back to wait for the others to join us. By five p.m. they had not shown up and the driver indicated that he would not wait any longer. To my surprise, Grant was happy to go and so leave Leslie behind. He never saw her again.

On the way back, Grant explained that he had tired of Leslie because she had become clingy and he had had enough of feeling responsible for her. I had noticed that she did not seem capable of making a decision without involving everyone else in the process and that sometimes this could get a bit tiresome. He was always non-committal and I got the impression that what Leslie really wanted was a bit of reassurance from Grant, who was just too laid back ever to give it. The episode of the ticket for the train was not so much that Grant was breaking hardcore traveller rules but that he tried to buy a ticket only for himself. I had assumed he had also tried to get one for Leslie and I must say I could see her point when he told me he had not. Having spent most of his adult life wandering around the world, I suppose he had become pretty self-centred. We discussed the meaning of the lyrics of the old Beatles' song but he had no comprehension of why Leslie had felt hurt. He also felt that the other hardened travellers did not like him and that Leslie was too anxious to please them.

I had seen them when they were both very happy together and found it odd, and a bit sad, that they should part so casually without even a goodbye. I didn't know it then, but I was going to bump into Leslie a few weeks later in Senegal, and I was going to hear the whole story again, but from her point of view. It was very different.

Chapter 5

Back at the campsite we chatted to a German with a very smart Land Rover who was leaving for Nouackshott in half an hour and Grant lost no time in cadging a lift. As usual he just took things as they came and as we waved him off I thought he had exactly the right approach for world travel. Enjoy the good times, take your opportunities, but don't get too upset when things go wrong because, sure as hell, they will.

That night Massami, Luc and I played cards, Grant rules, and Luc won every hand. As we played we watched enviously as the Dutch lady, Lise, who owned the place, knocked back a couple of decent looking bottles of red wine. We had not seen any alcohol since Morocco and would have loved to be invited to join her. Unfortunately, she explained that although she had a special dispensation to import wine, she would fall foul of the authorities if she either gave or sold it to her guests. I couldn't really blame her for not wanting to share the precious liquid with a passing bunch of alcohol-deprived travellers but when she staggered across to ask for a dance not one of us felt inclined to leave the card game. "You can drink alone but you can't party alone," sniffed Luc.

In the morning Massami and I packed up our bikes and set forth on the new tarmac road to Nouckshott. I didn't see Luc again but I met a Dutch motorcyclist in Ghana who rode with him for a while. He told me that Luc had met a local woman in Burkina Faso and had shacked up with her. I remembered a conversation back in Morocco between myself, Luc and a young Arab called Benny who owned the campsite on which we were staying. Benny asked Luc if he was married. Luc replied that he was not, in such a way that most Europeans would have dropped the subject. Arabs are much less reticent and he asked why not. Luc explained that his wife had died. Without taking a pause Benny asked how long ago. Four years. How did she die? A diving accident. I noticed that the more he was questioned in such a frank and uninhibited manner, the more Luc seemed to open up and he talked at some length about his life with his wife. He had clearly been traumatised by her death and he seemed to gain some comfort by having this opportunity to talk so openly.

Lise told us that we could expect a strong tail wind all the way and she was right. She showed no sign of a hangover and I guessed that her evenings often involved a couple of bottles. Still, she ran a great campsite in very inhospitable surroundings and I can't begrudge her a bit of alcoholic comfort.

The tarmac road had recently been built by the Chinese in return for fishing rights off the Mauritanian coast and it was immaculate. It was smooth as glass and with the tailwind we made excellent progress. Sand was being blown around but it was not too uncomfortable, as it was at our backs. This time I had stocked up with food and water and felt quite confident about reaching the town of Akjout, about 200 kilometres distant, without undue deprivation.

In the afternoon, after our customary three-hour stop in the middle of the day, Massami started to get recurring punctures. Whenever he got really frustrated he would emit a high-pitched screech rather like an excited parrot. This worked really well with over persistent kids who understandably got a bit frightened and soon left us alone. At the third puncture, the screech was beginning to frighten me as well and I consciously refrained from boasting that I had not had one puncture since leaving home. I had not even used my pump, but I kept my mouth shut tight.

At dusk we pushed our bikes a hundred metres from the road and set up camp. As I put up my tent in the near dark, I asked Massami why he was not putting up his. He replied that the moon would be up in twenty minutes and as it was going to be full, there would be more light if he waited. I asked him where it would appear and he pointed to a spot in the sky. Sure enough, twenty minutes later, the moon appeared exactly as he had predicted. In addition to his other skills, Massami was a very competent astronomer. For an hour or more he had me enthralled with an explanation of the constellations, made all the more absorbing, as the stars were so close and personal in the clear African sky.

As he prepared another wonderful meal, using tinned peas as a main ingredient because of the water and nutritional content, he confided that nobody knew he was in Africa. This staggered me because hundreds of people knew I was there and I couldn't understand how such a pleasant and fascinating bloke could be such an island. He had left his job and his flat in Dusselforf to go on this trip but had not told anyone because he did not plan to go back to the same town. He had been living in Germany for over twelve years, and so qualified for German citizenship, and had not seen his family back in Tokyo in that time. Sadly, he had been back to Tokyo, once to get parts for his beloved bike and once to attend the wedding of an old friend, but had not contacted his family on either occasion. Apparently, he was estranged from his family but it was only much later that I discovered why.

I got on really well with Massami and even though I was ten years his senior, he looked after me like his kid brother. He would never let me sit on the ground and always insisted that I use his portable chair. We were both happy to be together—he protected me from hunger and thirst and in return I protected him from the locals. It took a long time to come out but eventually I understood that Massami had been treated very badly by some of the people he had come across in Africa. With his exotic appearance and wonderful bike he attracted a lot of attention wherever he went. The kids would gather round him shouting questions, touching his bike and sometimes him.

Unfortunately, with no word of French and only rudimentary English, Massami could not communicate at all and the excitement quickly turned to hostility. There had been times when the kids had hit him with sticks, thrown stones at him and two adults on a motorbike had even tipped oil all over him. On one occasion he had been stopped by kids and youths in a mountain village and been forced to pay up or be beaten. He had to push his bike for two days when his rear wheel was wrecked by a stick rammed into the spokes. I had trouble from kids, especially in Morocco, but nothing compared with the aggression Massami experienced.

From time to time in the desert you get offers of hospitality from people; a cup of tea or just to sit with them in the shade. Massami always shunned these offers even though I was keen to accept, and I began to see why. I could also understand why he was so anxious to get a flight out of Africa and continue his cycle ride in Southern Europe. What a pity that such a friendly and generous bloke had met such hostility and ignorance. At least while he was with me it was easier to avoid trouble and I felt that I was able to give him something in return for everything he gave me.

When we parted several weeks later in Dakar, I asked him for his address but he did not have one. I asked if he wanted mine and he very politely said no and so, much to my regret, I will never see him again.

That night I awoke in my tent feeling very sick. I lay back hoping the feeling might pass but it only got worse. It always does. Eventually I knew that vomiting was inevitable and I crawled out of my tent. In the bright moonlight I staggered into the desert not knowing whether I would shit or vomit first. As it happens I did both simultaneously and with violent abandon. I was conscious of thinking it was lucky I was naked. On my hands and knees, I vomited over and over. It was heartbreaking to see Massami's nutritious peas splattered all over the sand, wasted, together with all that precious liquid.

Over the next few hours I was sick a few more times and although I began to feel a bit better, I was worried because during the course of the night I drank a lot of the water that I had put in reserve for the following day. At daybreak I decided to go and wait outside

Massami's tent so that when he woke I could tell him to go easy on his water, as he would have to share it with me. As the dawn broke, his tent zip was violently ripped open and he got his head out just in time to vomit just as enthusiastically as I had done a couple of hours earlier. We were both in the same boat and I smiled sympathetically at him and walked away to let him get on with it in a bit of privacy.

We had about fifty kilometres to cover to the next village and we were both feeling sick, weak and dehydrated. Between us we had about two litres of water, very little under the circumstances, and we decided that we should just pack our bikes and go for it. There was no alternative.

It was a miserable, silent ride and for once the tail wind failed us. Two or three hours later we could see Akjout in the distance and we pedalled with renewed heart. It was one of the grottiest and dirtiest of all the towns we had seen in Mauritania (which is saying something) and at first I was worried that it was deserted. Then we saw one of the Sahara's most welcome sights—a little shop advertising those ubiquitous desert staples, Coca Cola and Fanta. Inside the shop there was little apart from a huge fridge. A very pretty young girl, who was sitting among cushions on the floor, served us a couple of ice cold Fantas. She offered us some cushions and we sank to the floor, too exhausted to do anything other than sip our drinks. Much to the amusement of the girl we stayed there over an hour as the pile of empty cans grew. She was doing her homework and asked me to look at it. As I did so, various people put their heads through the door to have a look at the weird European cyclists who were drinking all the Coke and Fanta in the village. I told her I was very impressed with her homework; it was a very neat map of the country, with pictures of camels, palm trees and fish in the sea. She made the place look like paradise and it felt strange to realise that she was proud of the country which I had come to regard as a shit hole. I hope she got a good mark, if only for making me think again.

As we prepared to ride off a small crowd appeared and the girl gave us some little homemade biscuits. She must have taken a week's turnover in the hour we were there, and, once we were back in the desert, I had my first pee since leaving Atar.

The rest of the ride to Nouackshott was hard and tedious. The road is straight and although we were pleased that the wind had returned it also raised the sand so that we could never quite escape it. Had the wind been into our faces, we would never have made it. One of the features of desert life is that there is no shade and I found this hard to get used to. As soon as you stop, the flies appear from nowhere and batter your mouth and ears in their hunt for moisture. I wondered how flies could survive where there is nothing but sand and rock but they do. There is no scenery and with so much sand in the air, the sky is grey, not blue. The local people seemed to be as harsh and as inhospitable as their country and I had to keep reminding myself that there was at least one little girl who thought it was wonderful. The best time is early evening when the wind drops, the flies disappear and the stars come out.

It took us two more days to get to Nouackshott and by then I had practically recovered from the bug although whenever I ate I felt sick. Massami's response was typical of both his self-discipline and his no-nonsense approach—eat nothing for three days. So for three days his only sustenance was Coca-Cola, simple as that.

On Christmas Eve we were within striking distance of our destination and were looking for somewhere to shelter from the midday sun when we spotted an abandoned dwelling. These are great because they have holes built into the bottom of the walls to funnel the wind, so keeping you cool and discouraging the hateful flies. I was about to flop onto the floor when Massami gave me a warning shout— it was a small, pale scorpion with its tail arched just where I was about to sit. It was the first scorpion I had seen and it made my blood run cold; it just looked so deadly. Massami dispatched it without fuss.

As I sat in the shade, half asleep, I saw a small train of camels in the distance. Behind them on the horizon was a group of palm trees. The white sand was blowing over the road like snow and I fell into a reverie that I was in a Christmas card. Even the black bags blowing in the breeze could not break the spell.

On Christmas day we arrived at Nouackshott and found a campsite. Unfortunately it was locally run so it was dirty, fly blown and there was no water. It was also just down wind of a huge rubbish tip which burned day and night and gave me a sore throat. On the plus side it was next to a beautiful beach. Massami was still not eating and he spent the afternoon in his tent.

In the water-less toilet block I met the first Englishman I had seen in Mauritania. He was driving a car to Senegal to sell it and had done this several times before—he just loved driving through the desert. The thought occurred to me that he must be mad, which, on reflection, was a bit like the pot calling the kettle black. When I told him I was with Massami he said that he had heard about us and that the "English guy and the Japanese guy" were quite well known amongst the desert travelling community. I felt quite a celebrity until I realised that amongst this community everyone is aware of everyone else, and their particular mode of transport. During our ten-minute chat neither of us wished the other a Happy Christmas and in fact the subject wasn't even mentioned. Much as I hate the Christmas hype, being in a country where it simply does not exist made me feel a long way from home.

Massami was fast asleep and I cycled into the town to find a telephone to call my family. It was expensive but gave my spirits a huge lift, as I had not been able to contact them since Morocco. Talking to my son, I got the impression that he was a bit disappointed that I had "cheated" by catching the iron ore train. I tried to justify it on the grounds that the train had actually taken us farther away from our destination, but I guess in his position I would have felt the same.

I spent the afternoon on the beach watching the fishermen launch their boats through the surf. There was a crew of about six in each boat and about another ten women and children on the shore clinging to a rope to keep the bow of the boat pointing out to sea. It looked like hard work but everyone was cheerful and purposeful. Fish seemed to be plentiful and catches were loaded onto carts pulled by donkeys and then sold in a bustling market under a huge concrete shelter. It was a genuinely picturesque sight and there were stalls selling tea, bread and fried fish pieces. For once I was oblivious to the flies. There were virtually no tourists and it was nice therefore not be hassled. I must have stood out like a sore thumb but my presence did not give anyone a problem. A man in his early twenties struck up a conversation at a tea stall. He told me he had a small house in the town and also part owned one of the fishing boats on the beach. There were signs, even in this country, of a fledgling tourist industry and he was in two minds about whether to convert the house into a backpackers' hostel or to concentrate his energy and resources on fishing. Mauritania hasn't got much going for it, and it is hard to appreciate its strictly Islamic culture, but tourism will go there as it goes everywhere. The very inaccessibility of a country is a draw to people looking for somewhere different and exotic. He asked my opinion and I told him I would choose tourism but it depressed me to think that this beach would soon become a tourist trap with all the hassles and greed that goes with it. I asked a woman who was gutting fish and carrying on about fifteen simultaneous conversations if I could take her picture. She was delighted and her friends all gathered round to be included, shouting raucous and no doubt bawdy comments at me. As I said goodbye to them all I hoped that she wouldn't soon be charging the punters for their tourist snaps.

Back at the campsite, a huge marquee had been erected and I took a peek inside. The interior was laid out in preparation for a sumptuous banquet and I wondered if the planned party was anything to do with Christmas. The old lady who owned the site told me it was to honour her son who had returned home from studies abroad. It was clear that no expense had been spared and she had booked one of the best song and dance troupes in the region. I told her how much I admired her country and its music but still did not manage to elicit an invitation. As I walked back to tell Massami what I had learned, I consoled myself with the reflection that at least I would be able to listen to some Mauritanian music. Despite what I had said to the old lady, I had heard none so far and assumed it didn't exist.

That night I fell asleep listening to beautiful singing with complicated harmonies the like of which I had not heard since "Good Vibrations." I loved it but in the morning Massami complained bitterly that he had been kept awake all night. He obviously hadn't quite recovered from his illness.

As we rode south, heading for the border with Senegal at Rosso, the terrain became much more cycle friendly. There were trees and shade, and villages started appearing, so getting water became much easier. The only problem was a particularly vicious type of burr which managed to attach itself to you whenever you went into the bush to rest or to camp. Because they are covered in tiny barbs they are very uncomfortable for the skin and picking them off was really sore on the fingers, as they are both tenacious and very sharp. In Africa there is always something to complain about.

Massami and I were sharing a shelter with a couple of goats when we were joined by a small group of youths who seemed to be led by a particularly haughty Arab. He started asking me the usual questions about where we had come from and why were we not in a car. (As usual it was assumed we could not afford one.) However, he had a rather unfriendly aspect and I sensed that Massami, with his mistrust of all local people, was getting anxious for us to be on our way. Our interrogator shifted the conversation to Islam and asked why Westerners had no respect for his religion. He also wanted to know what was my religion. I explained that I had none but that I respected other peoples' religions. The atmosphere got tense and he said that the war in Iraq was proof that we did not respect Islam. I was also becoming keen to get away but did not want to appear worried or to be making a break for it. Joy had given me a little stick of lip salve to protect my lips from the desert sun and, for some reason, I pulled it out and started to apply it. The youths looked at me incredulously and then amid shrieks of "rouge a levres" (lipstick) they burst out laughing. I joined in and even Massami smiled as the tension drained away. Nonetheless the episode did nothing to lessen Massami's fear of local people and we never again stopped for shelter unless it was far from any sign of habitation.

It was late in the afternoon as we approached Rosso and we were told at a police roadblock that a Japanese girl on a motorbike was trying to find us. Sure enough a tiny figure on a huge trail bike roared alongside, just as we entered Rosso. In full riding leathers you could only see that Makikio was female when she took off her helmet. We were just in the process of introducing ourselves when we were mobbed by the most aggressive hustlers I ever encountered in Africa. Being a border town, Rosso has spawned a sub-industry of unofficial guides who take innocent travellers through the corruption and bribery which has to be negotiated to cross the river into Senegal. The three of us split up like islands in a flood and were surrounded by "guides" offering their services, touts shouting about the insurance they claimed we would need and others offering impossibly cheap deals on the river crossing. We literally could not move in this jostling mass of humanity and I shouted across to Massami and Makiko that we should retreat out of the town. Back on the road we decided to camp in the bush overnight and then try the crossing very early in the morning before the hustlers were up. We rode into the bush which was full of thorns and all three of us got punctures—for me this was the first puncture since leaving home.

It was great to have Makiko with us, as at last Massami could have a fluent conversation with someone. Speaking only German and Japanese, this was a rare opportunity in the Sahara. She could also translate for Massami and me and I was able to clear up a lot of the linguistic mysteries we had shared during our time together. In particular I was intrigued by why he had become so estranged from his family that he hadn't seen them for twelve years. It transpired that his parents had disowned him because had turned his back on Japan to claim German citizenship. They were very nationalistic, traditional people and I guessed that their free-spirited, unconventional son had probably crossed swords with them well before he developed a hankering to live in Europe. To me, Massami was an enigma—such a friendly, generous and interesting guy spurned by his family and without a friend in the world. Makiko and I swapped addresses and I have often been in e:mail contact with her but predictably Massami told her he had no address and he did not take hers. Reading between the lines, I think Makiko was a bit disappointed.

As we sat under the stars eating yet another superb Massami-meal, Makiko told us how she had left Japan on her motorbike and rode across Siberia into Scandinavia, then crossed Europe down to

Gibralter and so into Morocco and Mauritania. Her plan was to ride to Cape Town and then return up the East Coast of Africa, into the Middle East, Turkey and then back across Siberia to Japan. In all she had three years leave from the motorbike shop where she worked. At just under five feet tall, Makiko looked tiny beside her huge Suzuki 600 and she told us that when she was on her own she kept her helmet on while she put up her tent so that people would not see that she was a woman. At a hostel in Siberia a drunken Russian had tried to rape her but she had seen him off. Her courage and ambition just knocked me out, but she didn't seem to feel that she was doing anything special.

She had heard about the English and Japanese guys on bikes and decided to catch us up. She was thirty, Massami forty and I was fifty and Makiko reckoned the symmetry of our ages augured well for our friendship. She was right and we became quite close. Makiko was obsessed by motorbikes and I called her a petrol head. She reckoned we were air heads (having been blown across the Sahara by favourable winds).

At dawn we headed back into town but the hustlers were waiting for us and as they surged towards us we turned tail again and regrouped down the road. There was another border crossing about a hundred kilometres down the Senegal river and we decided to try our luck there. Makiko went off ahead saying that she would come back to us if it was not possible to cross, but all being well she would meet us in St Louis, the first town across the border in Senegal. I spent the morning trying to remember the plot line to *Meet me in St Louis*. Massami had never heard of the film and nor could he understand why the hell I was on about it.

According to Massami's map there was a little village on the track, midway to the border crossing, where we could stop for food and water. The track was a pleasure to cycle along, as it followed the course of the river, which was the first lying water we had seen since coming into the Sahara. It was surrounded by dense grassy vegetation teeming with birdlife. We were warned to watch out for wild boar and I was delighted to see one crossing the road in front of us—the first big wild creature I saw in Africa.

The village never materialised so by the end of the day when we got to the border crossing we were in our usual state—tired, hungry and thirsty. (We could not draw water from the Senegal River, as at this point it is saline and even my prized pump could not deal with salt.) As we neared the bridge to cross into Senegal a party of French tourists cheered our arrival and videoed us and our bikes. It was always the French who made the greatest fuss of the fact that you were on a very long cycle trip, and they always had a lot of questions. By contrast, most Americans that I met seemed to find the idea of a trans-African cycle ride neither impressive nor particularly interesting.

Because of the welcome we received from the French we managed to get over the border without having to pay a huge bribe to the border guards: we got away with only a couple of euros each. Not so the other travellers who were waiting to get across in their four by fours. Each had to pay a hefty bribe to the police and then to the customs. One indignant Dutchman came out of the customs office complaining that he had had to pay a hundred euros because the official had asked how much he had paid the police. The Dutchman told him a hundred euros and the customs guy then said, "Well if you can pay him a hundred euros, you can pay me a hundred euros too." One of the drivers outside in the queue suggested that they should band together and refuse to pay the bribe but the ones who knew Africa were lukewarm. Corruption runs so deep that to resist is just tilting at windmills. Yet again I heard the refrain, "Hey, this is Africa…"

Once into Senegal, the track deteriorated drastically and we were forced to push our bikes through deep sand, which ruled out any possibility of reaching St Louis that night and we camped in the bush, near to a couple of Germans in a camper van with a broken wheel. They had been waiting twenty-four hours for a friend to turn up with a replacement wheel and were so tired and demoralised that they did not even ask us what we were doing there.

We had bought water at the border and I was pleased not to be going to bed thirsty, only hungry, when Massami did his loaves and fishes trick and produced another meal out of thin air. Bread and tinned sardines had never tasted so good, and yet again I thanked my lucky stars that I had met Massami.

The next morning we said goodbye to the disconsolate Germans who were still waiting and pushed our bikes to a tarmac road and then crossed a bridge that had once spanned the Danube and entered the faded but beautiful town of St Louis. Set on the mainland, an island and then a thin spit of land all connected by bridges, the town is almost a caricature of a French colonial town and probably the most relaxed place in Africa. We crossed all the bridges to get to the spit and turned south to find a clean campsite on the edge of a vast unspoilt beach. There we found Makiko who had already got to know the other travellers, the usual mix of Europeans with a few Americans, Aussies and Kiwis. Some were in immaculate vehicles with the new style tents on the roof and others in old jalopies so decrepit that you wondered how they had made it through the desert. It was New Year's Eve and I had not had a drink for months, so when Makiko suggested that we go in search of some booze for a party I was all in favour. To get to the town centre we had to walk through the "fishing village" where mountains of fish were being dried and smoked by scores of women. In the light of the setting sun, with the smoke and the fires, the scene was eerie and almost biblical. The fish was distributed all over Senegal and even as far as Mali. Street traders sold pieces of deep fried fish in bread with a sprinkling of chilli pepper and this became my staple diet while I was in St Louis.

Leaving a store with a bag full of beer we bumped into Leslie. She had split from the hardcore travellers and was now staying on her own at a tourist hotel in the town. The others were staying at the home of someone whom they referred to as a friend but in fact was a local tout who had offered them cheap lodging. They were paying peanuts for the privilege of sleeping in the beds of his family and eating their food. She felt that the rest of the family had begun to resent having to do without their own beds and that they had probably outstayed their welcome. I remembered how hard they negotiated and reflected that rich western kids exploiting their superior economic strength was not a valid way of getting the "authenticity" they so craved. I invited her to our party and as we walked back to the campsite she told me about the last few days of her relationship with Grant, last seen on our day trip to Chinguetti in northern Mauritania. According to Leslie, he had become controlling and manipulative and she had needed to get away from him to retain her independence. As a single woman travelling across Africa, I could accept that Leslie would value her independence, and rightly so, but I just could not accept that Grant had a manipulative bone in his body. If anything, I think it irked her that he never offered an opinion when she sought his advice on what to do next. Leslie seemed to be permanently agonising over where to go and with whom whereas Grant always knew exactly where he was going. Leslie could come with him if she wished but he would never try to influence her decisions. Grant had the impression that the hardcore travellers didn't like him and Leslie confirmed this. They said he was arrogant and racist but reading between the lines, I took it that he took the piss out of their pretension and yes, he could be a bit non-PC at times.

As we walked, she told me that she had become disillusioned with travel and was thinking of going back home. Sure enough she asked me what I thought she should do. Perhaps a bit irritably I told her it was up to her. Much later on I felt obliged to walk her back to her hotel, as she claimed she was being hassled by local lotharios who hung around the hotel waiting for her. Well, they weren't there that day and as I walked all the way back again on my own I reflected that she had manipulated me into feeling responsible for her, the very complaint Grant had made.

Chapter 6

Senegal is an easy country to cycle through, reasonably flat with decent roads and easily accessible water. The people are friendly and all the kids get wildly excited when you pass through their villages. Even as you approach you hear the familiar shrieks of "Toubab, Toubabou!" as the children leave their games to race to the road to wave and dance. As we cycled south towards Dakar, and the airport, I hoped that Massami might be softening his attitude to Africa and change his mind about flying back to Europe. Camping in the bush was hassle free, there was plenty of firewood and getting food and water was easy. As we got nearer to Dakar, though, the people seemed to change; the begging became more aggressive and the roads became clogged and dangerous. As I had feared, it was all too much for Massami and he confirmed that he wanted to leave as soon as he could get a ticket. We struggled through the miles and miles of gridlocked vehicles, all spewing noxious fumes that turned our throats red raw, and found a little campsite to the north of the city, quite close to the airport.

I needed a visa for my next country, Burkina Faso, and Massami wanted a plane ticket so we decided to take a bus rather than ride into the city. Cycling was just too dangerous and unpleasant. The next morning we were at the bus stop waiting for the first bus, and were pleasantly surprised to find that it was almost empty. We paid our fares as we entered and took our seats and settled back to enjoy the ride into the city. After a few stops the bus started to fill and soon we were stuck in stationary traffic. The sun began to beat against the window next to me and, as more passengers boarded the bus, they were forced to stand in the aisle which was getting packed. A group of women dumped their bags on our laps and the crush in the aisle became so intense that standing people were leaning on those with seats. Still the driver stopped for more passengers who were shoe horned into the bus. I had started taking my anti-malarial drug Larium a few weeks previously and I had read that one of the long list of side effects was anxiety and panic attacks. As my head became jammed against the window and I realised that I could not move, I thought it was a good job I was not prone to panic attacks. Just as I thought that, I wondered if I could get out if the bus was in an accident and toppled over. My chest started to tighten and I felt myself slip into panic. What made things worse was that we were in extremely heavy traffic and were stationary for long periods of time. I could not see Massami, even though he was sitting next to me, and I realised I would have to survive this situation on my own. I tried to calm myself down by breathing deeply but all I really wanted to do was to get off the bus. The Embassy closed at twelve midday so even if I could have managed to get off, it would mean I could not get there on time. We had already been on the bus for over an hour and did not appear to be anywhere near the centre. It was all I could do to sit still and not start screaming. I vowed that I would never again forsake the comfort and convenience of travelling by bike.

Gradually the passengers started to disembark and I recovered some of my composure. We got off at a city centre street and realised that by chance we were on the same street as the Embassy. Feeling a lot better, we found the address without too much trouble. There were a lot of flags and military personnel, just like all the government buildings, and I was relieved that we had been so lucky, as it was only an hour short of midday. I explained to a group of soldiers what I wanted and was directed to a reception area. There I had to show my passport and was directed to an office on the third floor. At this office I was told to join a short queue of local people in an anteroom and I began to worry about the time again. When I was called, I explained that I wanted a visa for Burkina Faso but was told by the officer that I did not need one. As we were speaking in French, I wondered if I had misunderstood him and I asked him to explain. He said that with my British passport I could cross into Burkina Faso without a visa. He said he was certain about this and dismissed me by nodding at the door.

Back in the anteroom I was explaining the events to Massami, who was very doubtful about what I had been told, when a local woman behind me in the queue called me over. In English, she told me that this building used to be the Burkina Faso Embassy but had recently become a local administration office. Incredibly, we were in the wrong place. She gave the new address of the B F Embassy and suggested we take a taxi straight away, as it was due to close at twelve. It was now a quarter to twelve and we hailed a taxi outside and I asked the driver how long it would take to get to the address. He said five minutes, and sensing my anxiety, quoted a huge fee which I accepted without demur. Leaping out of the taxi at the embassy, we met three travellers we had partied with on New Year's Eve in St Louis, two French-Canadian girls and a Frenchman, Francois, in a very smart Land Rover. Seeing I was in a hurry they shouted good luck as I dashed inside, where I was given a form to complete. I took it to a female officer who asked me for twenty-two thousand CFA. I said I only had fifteen and was just about to go and borrow some more money from Massami when she said it would do and I was to come back in two days to collect the visa in the afternoon. I had been told so many times that they were closed in the afternoon that I asked her to confirm she meant the afternoon. Rather irritably, she said if I came in the morning I would not get it.

Massami and I spent the afternoon buying a plane ticket for Tunis from where he planned to take a ferry to Sicily and then ride to Italy, Greece and Turkey. I tried to tell him that it would be cold and dark in Europe but he was set on quitting Africa. To protect his beloved bike on the flight he wanted to get some cardboard to construct a box and

I thought we would be able to get some for free at any TV or white goods shop in the city. I had forgotten that in Africa everything is recycled and nothing is for free, and we were quoted outrageous prices for old cardboard boxes at all the retailers. As always, when you are looking to buy something, a small crowd formed, hoping to make a buck out of the situation. Eventually we were taken to a back street where there was a huge pile of cardboard and Massami selected some good quality pieces. He was getting a lot of pressure from the guys clamouring to do business with him and I could hear the old parrot screech beginning to take form. I tried to bargain for a decent price but Massami was happy to pay way over the odds—it was for his bike after all. He also needed some tape and the same trader sold him this as well.

Rather than take the bus back to the campsite, we decided to patronise our sworn enemy, the mini-bus. All over Africa these vehicles are the scourge of cyclists. If someone invented a computer game about getting from Manchester to Cape Town by bike, the baddies would be touts, police and mosquitoes but the real monsters would be mini-buses. They are driven by psychopaths, invariably in a dangerous state of disrepair and belch enormous quantities of black smoke. Each one has an acrobatic exhibitionist who hangs onto the vehicle shouting and gesticulating at pedestrians in an attempt to secure as many passengers as possible. He also collects the fares, which are minimal, and provides a conductor service which is also minimal. There is intense competition to get to passengers first and the drivers are so highly motivated that nothing, least of all a cyclist, is allowed to get in the way. My worst nightmare was to be caught up in a group of these mini-buses as they weave in and out like Formula One drivers and suddenly veer in to the curb to shove in another passenger. In some areas they are emblazoned with religious slogans like "In God We Trust" and some have darkly humorous names like "Death or Glory" or "Prepare for Death." They are noisy, dirty and dangerous and the effect they have is to heighten the anxiety level of all other road users. The reason why road traffic statistics are so horrendous in Africa is because when these taxis crash, the death toll is invariably high.

We found the mini-bus station for our area and in the inevitable chaos and confusion we eventually boarded a bus which we were told was going our way. Putting destination indicators on the buses would reduce some of the confusion but it is not done, it would just be too easy.

Our "conductor" took Massami's cardboard and tied it to the roof, charging a small premium on our fare. It was the end of the day and in ten minutes the bus was crammed and we set off. As we pulled out of the station onto the main road the bus ground to a halt; it had broken down. Nobody complained as we were shepherded off and into another bus and the cardboard was transferred at no extra cost. Planks of wood had been placed over the aisle to create extra seats, and a youngster leaned over and asked why we were taking this form of transport rather than a taxi. I told him we could not afford a taxi but he did not believe me which was hardly surprising, as it was not true. He was bright and friendly and had a job with a local paper where he hoped to become a journalist. With his approach I could see him succeeding, and I would have enjoyed talking to him at greater length but the bus lurched to another halt with a punctured tyre. It came as no surprise to see that we had no spare and the passengers climbed out while we waited for some unspecified solution. Still nobody complained. By now there would be serious grumbling if this had been Britain and raised voices, at least, in France. In Africa people were much more stoic, as if their expectations are just so much lower. I had noticed this many times before—a person waiting for a bus to fill before it departed never seemed to get impatient. They just switch off and wait. They don't fidget or sigh, it is almost like suspended animation. I still can't decide if this trait is admirable or deplorable, but it doesn't get things improved. I am unsure how this characteristic sits with the tendency of African states to change their regimes frequently and violently.

Eventually the spare tyre arrived and we piled back into the bus. Five minutes later the tyre was flat again and Massami and I decided we were close enough to walk and I climbed onto the roof to retrieve his cardboard. We could see the lights of the airport and knew that all we had to do was walk to the other side. Our young friend could not understand our impatience and warned us it was still a long walk and it was already dark. Half an hour later the bus caught up with us and he leaned out the window suggesting we get back on. For some reason we both declined, maybe something to do with a reluctance to eat humble pie. We then got seriously lost in the shantytown surrounding the airport and nearly three hours later we staggered into our campsite.

The three people we had met at the Embassy turned up the next morning, as we had told them it was a good place to stay, apart from the hundreds of cats who pissed on our tents and fought all night. Unfortunately the site was in a compound and it was not possible to get in with their Land Rover. Reluctant to leave it outside for security reasons they went in search of another site. I never saw the two Canadian girls again but did bump into Francois in a Catholic Mission in east Senegal a couple of weeks later.

Massami was hard at it building a magnificent reinforced cardboard box and I wandered off to the beach to watch the fishermen launching their blue and white pirogues through the white surf. As always it was a picturesque scene but I had been warned that muggings were common and it was not safe to stray too far. In the distance I saw the outline of a lone woman striding confidently along the beach. She was in hardcore traveller dress, a style mix of safari and native, and had evidently come from the area I had been advised to avoid. As she approached I greeted her and she came over to chat. She was in her sixties and a German teacher who liked to spend her holidays travelling to exotic locations. From time to time I met ladies like this travelling alone in Africa, independent and impervious to danger. She smiled knowingly when I said that I had been warned against walking where she had just come from. It might be dangerous for a nervous little tourist like me, she seemed to be thinking, but I am a hardened traveller.... Invariably ladies of this ilk love everything they see and everyone they meet and it seems everyone loves them. I never knew whether to envy them or pity them, but I always disliked being patronised by them. I related the story of our aborted minibus trip the previous day and she topped it with a description of a similar journey she had taken where things had gone so wrong that a four-hour trip eventually took all day and all night. I fell into the trap of expressing sympathy but she retorted with the standard hardcore traveller line: "Oh not at all, it was a fantastic experience...."

Back at the campsite Massami was still working on his box. I had to say it was a magnificent job; he had even constructed triangular struts which he inserted into the corners to add strength. It was so like Massami to take such care and so unlike me—I would have done the job at the airport and then ask them nicely to be careful with it. Naturally he wouldn't let me help him and as I watched, a young girl who hung around the site but didn't seem to work there, wandered over and asked if I would give her one of my oranges. As she ate the orange, spitting the pips flirtatiously at Massami, who was not amused, she asked if I liked Choff. This is a fish delicacy, famous in the area, and I had not tried it yet. She said that for 15000 CFA she would make us a Choff dinner at her home. I was keen but Massami, who had not lost his suspicion for local people, agreed only reluctantly.

Joola and I then entered negotiations and we agreed a final price of ten thousand CFA of which five thousand was to be up front so she could go and buy the fish. I gave her the money and she said she would be back at five. By six there was no sign of her and I knew what Massami was thinking, and to be honest, I was thinking the same. As the box was finished I wanted to take a picture of it against the background of the fish market just outside. I asked a youth who was hanging around if he would take the picture of Massami and me with the box. To my surprise he just said no and turned away. I took it myself and in the background I saw Joola waving at me. She was chatting with a group of women who were gutting fish and called me over like a long lost friend. She didn't seem to understand, or care, why I was confused that she had not showed up at five and proudly showed me the fish she had bought for our dinner. It was beginning to dawn on me that in Africa there is nothing to be gained from trying to make specific arrangements when only the broad outline will ever be adhered to. Joola always meant to make us dinner but the bit about calling for us at five was just a sop to the European obsession for tacking a time onto everything.

Ten minutes later the three of us were walking up the sandy road to go to her house when she asked for five hundred CFA to get a taxi. Massami told me to tell her we had both assumed she lived within walking distance and that we were not prepared to take a taxi. He was still sure that Joola wasn't quite kosher and I also was beginning to have reservations. I explained all this to Joola and she said not to worry, she would pay the fare. At the end of the street was a taxi and we all piled in for a five minute ride to her house. It transpired that the taxi driver was Joola's father and naturally enough she was just trying to make an extra five hundred CFA. In the taxi Joola asked for the balance of the agreed payment and I said we would pay when we had eaten the meal. She seemed to find our suspicions highly amusing and was not at all offended.

The house was in a small clump of nicely appointed buildings and Joola showed us around, including the kitchen on the second floor where she was going to cook our fish.

Apart from a few young toddlers, the house was full of pretty girls about the same age as Joola, all introduced either as sisters or friends. We were then shown into Joola's room where we were to wait until our dinner was ready. The room was obviously a girl's bedroom with lots of teddy bears and pink hairbrushes with a huge bed and nowhere to sit. I had never seen Massami looking so uncomfortable and I was beginning to feel guilty about getting him into this situation. If he had said he wanted to leave I would not have argued.

We sat stiffly on the edge of the bed and waited for whatever was coming next. It was Joola and to my relief she carried a silver tray on which were two plates of fish. There were no vegetables and we ate off our laps but the fish was delicious. Even Massami was happy and began to relax. Joola stood watching us eat with a smile that said weren't we silly to be so suspicious.

After we had eaten, I paid the money and included a hefty tip. Joola showed us out and gave us both a peck on the cheek. The neighbours gave us a long hard look as we walked out but neither of us cared. I tried to explain the old football insult about not being able to score in a brothel to Massami. He didn't understand but we had a good laugh on the way back home.

On the day that I was to pick up my visa Massami and I decided to cycle in to the embassy and we were rewarded with a glorious ride along a coastal road which took us no more than thirty minutes. We recycled a conversation we had many times—that the best way to travel in Africa is by bike. This conversation was so familiar, and our lines so well rehearsed, that Massami's lack of English was barely noticeable and that was probably another reason to recycle it.

I had been told to collect my visa in the afternoon but suspected that the office was only open in the morning, so we arrived at ten a.m. to be safe. It was ready and waiting for me and just to satisfy my curiosity I asked the receptionist whether they were open in the afternoon. He replied that they opened only in the morning and pointed to a notice on the wall confirming this. Having gone to some lengths to question the instruction to collect the visa in the afternoon, I left the building feeling quite indignant, as I could so easily have wasted a day and maybe that was the intention. It fell to Massami to remind me that this was Africa and that if you tried to get to the bottom of every mystery you would soon go mad.

As he was due to fly to Tunis the next day, Massami wanted to have a look round Dakar. We had a cheboujienne lunch in a little café near the market and then walked to the main square because Massami had decided he wanted to take me for a proper cup of tea, as it was our last day together. Tea had become something of a ritual for us in the desert, and Massami had introduced me to the pleasures of tea mixed with marmalade. Needless to say, he carried an array of jams and conserves in his saddlebags.

We found a smart tourist café rather than the locals-only type of establishment we normally used. It was very nice to be served at a table, and to order from a menu, but we had been on the road for quite awhile and I was conscious of the staff being a bit sniffy. Waiters know instinctively if you are getting above your station. Nonetheless I enjoyed the clean surroundings and I had a fabulous pot of Earl Grey.

And it was a nice change to use a loo that didn't involve having to go outside.

Afterwards, as we crossed the square, I became conscious of a guy close on my left while a guy on my right put his hand on my arm and showed me a single item of jewellery on a piece of brown paper. I recognised this immediately as a prelude to a robbery attempt and turned to the guy on my right and shouted, "Get your fucking hands off me or I'll fucking knife you!" He gesticulated with his head to his mate and they both walked quickly away. My outburst had been completely spontaneous and so totally out of character that even I was surprised. God knows why I threatened him with a knife, as I didn't have one, but I knew I would have hit the guy had he not backed off. Whilst I was pleased that the episode had ended as it did, I wondered if my reaction might have been down to the Larium rather than any newfound confidence in my street fighting skills. Massami thought it was something in the Earl Grey, but on reflection I thought it was probably down to both the Larium and the tension caused by the constant need to keep my antennae alert to the threat of robbery. I made a mental note to remember that aggression is not always the smartest response to these situations, and I wouldn't always get away with threatening to fucking knife people. Especially as I don't carry one.

The next day Massami packed his bike carefully into the box and for good measure tied rope round the package like a ribbon. I had assumed that we would carry it to the airport and that I would see him off there but he had ordered a taxi and I had time just to shake his hand before he was away. I had decided to give him a present of a fluorescent cycle belt which I thought would be useful in cold and dark Europe, but he just smiled and said he didn't want it. I was used to Massami's ways and didn't feel offended. When I next went into my tent I found a box of Earl Grey tea bags (where on earth had he found those?) and his map of Africa. He was an enigma and I didn't feel it was essential to understand him to like him.

I remembered one of our roadside camps when we had been about to start eating an evening meal. A young lad pushed his bike to us and asked me if I knew how to fix his brakes. I said sorry, I was not a mechanic. Firstly, I was just about to eat and was hungry. Secondly whenever you work on a bike your hands get oily and, living in a tent, it is very difficult to get them clean again. Thirdly, I really could not be bothered. Massami put down his food, took a look at the bike and then went to get his tools. To fix the bike properly he had to use a spare cable he had carried all the way from Germany, and by the time he got to his food it was stone cold. Yet it was kids like this who had made his life miserable and had been largely responsible for his decision to quit Africa.

I also knew that he did not want to exchange addresses, so did not offer. We had been together for about eight weeks and it seemed too final to part without the possibility that we would ever meet again. Later I realised that of course he was quite right—we could never have held a meaningful telephone conversation as we could barely understand each other face to face. With hours to spare, under the stars in the desert, we managed to convey some meaning but on the phone it would be impossible. Likewise, as two cyclists crossing the desert we had loads in common and our friendship was natural and spontaneous: back home in Manchester it might have been very different, so why take the risk?

Chapter 7

Even when you get on as well as I did with Massami, there is always a price to pay for companionship in that you have to give up some of your autonomy. Being with someone gives you security and confidence, and you avoid the numbing loneliness which used to descend on me whenever I had been completely alone for a week or so. But I was always pleased to get my independence back whenever I parted from my latest travelling companion.

There is an island off Dakar called Isle de Goree, which Massami was not keen to visit because it is a tourist trap but which I decided, post-Massami, that I wanted to see. It was only a short ferry ride across the bay and as I disembarked with the other tourists, we were greeted by a gaggle of touts offering rooms in their houses. I declined all the offers and one guy patiently explained to me that unless I stayed at the expensive hotel, there was nowhere else to stay, and the last ferry of the day had gone. Little did he know that strapped to the back of my bike I had a tent. Little did I know that on the tiny island there's just about nowhere to put it.

The main draw to the island was an old slave house which had an exit built into a seaward wall through which the slaves left Africa for America. It is a UNESCO World Heritage site and a tour round it is a very moving experience. It was only much later that I discovered that it was mainly a sham and that, whilst a few slaves had been held on the island, none had left from there. The myth was perpetuated in order to lure rich African Americans in search of their roots away from the genuine slave forts in Ghana and Ivory Coast, so that they spent their tourist dollars in Senegal. Massami had got it right again.

Amongst a series of gun emplacements, at the top of the island lived a community of Baye Fall hippies who made their living selling art and craft pieces to the tourists. I asked a group of them if it was OK to camp for the night and they said fine but quoted me a ripoff figure. Disillusioned but not too surprised, I wandered back down the hillside; there weren't any places to pitch a tent. An old man tending a small herd of goats said he had never seen a bicycle on the island, and we started to chat. He asked me where I was staying and I told him I was looking for somewhere to camp, whereupon he took me to a little plot of land where he kept his goats. It was on the side of the hill and sloping more steeply than was comfortable, but it was perfect for a panoramic view across the bay. I put up my tent, watched the sun set and went to bed. For the only time in Africa, I managed to get the BBC World Service on my radio and I fell asleep listening to *Westway*. Only committed insomniacs know this weird radio soap which always seems to feature an argument between two guys with broad Jamaican accents and someone called Joy who keeps getting dumped on. Back home I was a regular listener although I would struggle to describe a single plot line, but I felt comforted by its familiarity.

In the morning, waiting for the ferry back to the mainland, I wandered round the stalls selling arts and crafts. They were all manned by women, which was unusual, and they had a strangely coquettish sales pitch. Some of the artwork was interesting and if you stopped for a look the women would ask your name and tell you their own. Before you could move on they would extract a promise that you would come back to their stall. It was all hugely flirtatious and a bit theatrical, but I was happy to enter into the spirit of the game and give my promise. However, when I went to get on the ferry, one of them followed me and, apparently distraught, harangued me as if I had just jilted her. She even managed to make me feel guilty and I hoped that after I was out of sight she had a good laugh with her mates; in fact I'm sure she did.

I fought my way through the usual chaos in Dakar and, heading east towards Mali on a modern dual carriageway, I came upon a huge traffic jam. There was absolutely no oncoming traffic and the traffic on my side was stationary. Clearly there was a major blockage and up ahead, in the distance, I could see an ominous pall of smoke. Most people were standing in groups on the side of the road, just like they do when the M6 snarls up. Seeing a knot of white guys in loud clothing, I pulled over to ask if they knew what was going on. They were American ex pats, working in some capacity for the diplomatic service. The one I spoke to was arrogant and patronising and, using pretty undiplomatic language, he told me that a few miles ahead was a village where a cement factory had just announced its closure. The factory was the major employer in the region and the local people were understandably upset. In protest they had barricaded the road which was the main east – west trunk in Senegal. The Americans were on a day off and had planned to go fishing until they were thwarted by the roadblock. I couldn't resist remarking that it was a pity they weren't on bikes. They suggested that for my own safety, I should turn back and get out of the area before the army arrived to break it up. There was no way I could give them the satisfaction of seeing me turn around and I wished them luck in getting to their fishing trip and set off towards the billowing smoke. I felt nowhere near as confident as I hoped I looked.

As I got into the village, I could see the road had been blocked by huge rocks and slabs of concrete. In the gloom created by the black smoke of dozens of burning tyres a large crowd had formed. Sections of the crowd were toi toing which is a rather sinister-looking dance performed whenever there is trouble. I wondered how people would react to the idea of a white man on a bicycle crossing their roadblock. The atmosphere was tense but to my surprise, my arrival was greeted with a huge cheer. I smiled back, got off the bike and picked my way through the fires and rocks. My presence seemed to generate amusement rather than hostility. There was no sign yet of the police or army, but it was obvious they were expected and, as my American friend had suggested, things could get nasty when they arrived. I decided not to hang around.

At the other side of the roadblock was the start of another long queue of traffic but I had my side of the road to myself and it was very pleasant to cycle along the road without having to worry about dodging traffic coming from behind. It was at least an hour before I started to be overtaken, and I reckoned this was by vehicles that had turned back in despair.

My satisfaction at having been probably the only person to make it through that village was tempered somewhat when I saw a sign indicating that I was heading for a town due north of my destination. Later, when I studied Massami's map, I realised that in the excitement I had taken a wrong turning at the roadblock and that mistake took me at least a day's ride out of my way.

As I had plenty of time it was no great disaster to get lost, which was just as well as, despite Massami's map and a good compass given to me by a friend in the U.K., it was not uncommon.

On one occasion I realised that I was on the north side of the River Niger when I had spent the day thinking I was to the south. Another of my rules, like always to accept offers of hospitality, was never to retrace my steps, and I don't think I ever did. So I carried on following the north bank of the river hoping to come across a village where I might be able to find a boat to get me over. It was very rare to meet other cyclists but two French guys appeared heading in the other direction. They were riding from Ghana to France and had a web site, for which they took a photo of me and the bike. They gave me the web address on a business card which unfortunately was taken with my rucksack in Mozambique. All I remember about these guys was that they were both incredibly tall, and they told me that a few kilometres ahead was a pirogue which would take me and the bike across the river.

Sure enough, at an incredibly beautiful section of river, I came across a tiny hamlet and a small group of people waiting for the pirogue which was in the middle of the river. This was the first habitation I had seen for hours and I was relieved to see that they had a well, as my water supply was running low. As usual the men were sitting in the shade and the women were in the queue for water, but unusually they did not seem terribly friendly when I asked for permission to use the well. The women in the queue, normally so garrulous and ribald, were quiet, even sullen as I filled my six-litre plastic bag. Even the kids, who normally mobbed me, seemed reluctant to approach and in this remote region, I started to feel a little unwelcome.

At first the pirogue owner balked at the prospect of transporting my bike although eventually he relented but charged more for the bike than for me. On the boat I felt very uncomfortable and imagined that the people were talking about me. Right in front of me were two youths who seemed particularly unfriendly and kept looking at the large bags on my bike. I just couldn't wait to get off the boat and pedal as fast as possible away from this apparently blighted area.

My throat was parched and in preparation for the riding to come, I decided to have a drink. It's quite tricky to drink directly from a six-litre container but I was doing OK until the shoulder of the bag suddenly burst and nearly six litres of water cascaded over my head and soaked me to the skin.

I really felt that I had had enough and not for the first time wished I had never left home. One of the youths in front of me half smiled and feeling silly I smiled back. His mate laughed aloud and suddenly I was laughing and then the whole boat was laughing. It was full bodied, tear jerking laughter that lasted for easily five minutes and surely could be heard on both banks of the Niger. Even the pirogue owner had to put down his oars as he clutched his head and convulsed. The tension dissolved and by the time we got to the shore, I had explained to everyone that I had cycled from England and that I was married and had two children and that I was going to South Africa. As usual I was asked which was my favourite country and as usual it was the one I was in. Getting out of the boat was much easier than getting in, as everyone wanted to help lift out the bike.

The two youths were brothers whose family ran a small trading shop across the river where they took me for a cup of tea and a long chat about how poor the area was and how they valued their education, which their father paid for by working long hours in the shop. With my suspicious mind I thought they were leading up to a request for financial assistance with their education, but this did not materialise. Instead, I bought some provisions from the shop and I had to insist very hard before they would let me pay for them. Even then they chucked in a bunch of bananas for which they flatly refused to take payment.

Chapter 8

Heading towards the Senegal/Mali border, I stopped to eat an orange under a thatched roadside shelter. A strikingly good-looking guy with dreadlocks pulled up in a gaily painted, very old American Army Jeep and joined me under the shelter. I offered him half my orange and he told me he was called Jean and he lived in the Baye Fall hippy commune on Isle de Goree. He spoke French in such a way that I did not have too much trouble understanding him, probably because he had spent some time in France where he had met his current girlfriend. He was taking the Jeep to a vehicle market in the next town where he expected to secure a better price than he would get in Dakar. As I got up to go, Jean said as we were going to the same place, why not chuck my bike in the back and take a lift from him?

When I had first left the U.K. it had never occurred to me that I would ever accept lifts in any circumstances, and in Morocco I often declined a lift up a hill or when I was pushing the bike. Occasionally I would feel a bit churlish but, after all, the idea was to cycle to South Africa, not to fraternise with the enemy and their internal combustion engines. However, as I approached the Sahara desert, I struck up a friendship in a campsite with an elderly Frenchman and his relatively young wife who invited me to have dinner with them.

Gerard and Krystyna were a lovely couple and I had a great

evening with them. I told them I was heading south to Sid Ifni and they told me they were heading east. The following morning I was having a coffee with Luc, the Belgian guy on a motorbike and Benny, the owner of the site. Gerard walked over and with a huge grin told me that he and Krystyna had decided to go to Sidi Ifni and would I go with them. It was only about 50 kilometres but I had come all this way on my bike and I really did not want to break my purist record. Just in time, I saw that he was trying to do me a favour and my refusal would be a rebuff, particularly in front of the others, and I said that I would be delighted. As we drove off with my bike in the back it felt really strange to be in a vehicle after all that time, and I really enjoyed the ride. The only thing that bothered me was that whenever we stopped, Gerard would hand out sweets to the kids and I remembered how this expectation, which this type of behaviour helps to engender, had given me problems when I had nothing to give out. Some weeks later when I bumped into Luc in Mauritania, he took the piss unmercifully and thereafter he always referred to me as "Autostop," (the hitchhiker).

So when Jean offered me a lift, I did not feel I was breaking any personal rules, and I was so intrigued by his view of the world that I wanted to listen to some more. He had a theory that the African is like a tree whose roots do not allow him to move and it is for this reason that he will never make progress or better himself. In the region of the Baobab tree, venerated for all that it gives to man, it is not disparaging to talk in these terms and Jean did not think this was necessarily a bad thing—but it did explain, in his opinion, why the African had developed a dependency culture. Like a tree, he needs his food and water to be brought to him. Jean himself was an exception, as he had travelled extensively. He also spoke at some length and with great passion and lucidity about the damage done to Africa by the International Monetary Fund and the World Bank. He felt these organisations were a neo-colonialist plot to force developing nations into inappropriate economic measures of benefit only to the West and America in particular. The people who suffered the most were the poor because their governments were obliged to keep interest rates high and were severely discouraged from spending money on education, housing and health. Whereas Africa has a crying need for "big" government, the IMF wanted to impose the ultra liberalism of "little" government. Where their fledgling economies need careful protection and nurturing (like Japan and the other Asian tigers used to enjoy), they get the brutalities of global free trade. I had heard of the riots at G8 conferences around the world but had never really appreciated the background until meeting Jean. Having spent so much time trying to put my finger on what was wrong with Africa, it came as a shock to learn so much in just a couple of hours. To this day, I am angered by the greedy and callous way that the West continues to exploit Africa through the offices of the IMF and World Bank.

The prospect of a lift was also appealing because that morning I had stopped at a roadside stall for "Toubab coffee" and I had been told that there was a group of French cyclists about three hours up ahead and I was trying to catch them. In fact they had spent the night camping at the church of the coffee seller. Toubab coffee is a deliciously strange brew which always gave me a lift and made me feel slightly pissed at the same time. I never really understood what was the magic ingredient, but whenever I asked for it I got knowing smiles and ice-breaking amusement.

Twenty minutes later, just as we were approaching the town, we overtook the three French guys. I waved at them from the window and they waved back, just as you do all day long when on a bike. It gave me some pleasure to note that they were on ordinary bikes with huge loads and were dressed in ordinary clothes—these were guys I could probably keep up with. In the town I bought Jean a coke, which to my disappointment he said was not enough and he wanted some money as well, and then I sat down to wait for the Frenchmen.

As they rode up they were chatting away but when they saw me they came straight over and we shook hands enthusiastically and introduced ourselves. They were all 22 years old and two of them, Severin and Alex, were students and the third, Francois, was a carpenter. Severin and Alex had ridden from Nantes and been joined by Francois who had flown to Dakar to meet up with them to cycle to Bamako. At Bamako they were to work as volunteers for six weeks at an SOS Village, a French charity looking after orphaned children. After this, Severin and Alex were to fly to South America where they planned to cycle to another SOS Village in Brazil. Francois was to fly back home to return to his job. None of them spoke English and I was happy at the prospect of improving my French. They were practising Catholics and, rather than spending their nights in the bush, they would seek out churches or Catholic schools where they asked permission to camp.

They were as keen for me to join them as I was and the four of us set off for the local Catholic Mission. The Father was not around to ask if we could camp in the grounds and an underling invited us to wait outside the rather grand house. He told us that all the guest rooms were vacant and that we could probably stay in some of them. When the Father arrived he did not seem very happy to see us but under the circumstances he agreed to let us camp but did not want us to use the guest rooms " in case someone else arrived."

Our rather cool reception did not go down well with my new friends and they remarked on the brand new Toyota in which the Father had arrived and the very fancy Sony TV and video we had seen in the house. We put up our tents and went to ask if we could leave our bikes on the verandah while we went into the town to buy some food. To add to the disappointment, we interrupted the Father and his staff at one of the most sumptuous meals I have ever seen in a private home, but were not invited to join them.

They were a great bunch of lads and we spent the next couple of days cycling through the Baobab savannah of eastern Senegal to the Mali border. The prevailing wind was into our faces so for the first few hours I struggled to keep up with them and at our first break I told them I was going to part company. Severin wouldn't hear of it and Francois immediately offered to carry my water bottles. Feeling both guilty and grateful I allowed him to carry my water from then on. Severin even devised a formation which allowed me to slipstream behind them. Although they denied it, the pace slowed and I was soon comfortable with the new arrangements. Their philosophy of cycling was directly opposite to Massami's. They used a bicycle because it was the easiest way to meet local people en route. Massami used a bicycle because he loved cycling—meeting local people was just an attendant hazard, to be avoided wherever possible.

Severin and Alex both had straggly black beards because they had vowed not to shave until they reached their final destination. The three of them were friends from their school days although I got the impression that Francois was a bit of an outsider. One night we decided to camp in the bush, as the nearest village was a long way off. In the distance we could see a fire which was a feature of the slash-and-burn cultivation practised by local farmers. Francois felt we should not camp in the vicinity, as the fire would drive snakes in our direction. The other two thought this was preposterous and neurotic (although I must admit it struck a cord with me). They told me that Francois had always been a worrier and implied that he was a bit soft for the rigours of the outdoor life in Africa. He was very artistic and most evenings, around the fire, he would get out a harmonica and provide some welcome background music.

Severin was the undoubted leader of the group, a tall dark and rather intense man with strong religious convictions who was dumbfounded, and saddened, that religion had no place in my life. He never tried to proselytise but we had some deep and interesting conversations on the meaning of life and all that, a great way to pass the time on a long bike ride. I became very fond of Severin over the next few weeks but sometimes I felt that he took too many of the world's cares onto his shoulders. Much later I was delighted to learn that, much to Alex's disgust, he had shaved off his awful beard after a young French girl at Bamako Catholic Mission had taken his fancy. He must have lightened up a bit.

Alex was the joker and, although I never got close to him, I soon became sufficiently accepted to become the butt of some of his jokes. He was a great mimic and he had us all in stitches when he took off my broken French and "foreign" mannerisms. I tend to use "*n'est-ce pas*" rather a lot and Alex reckoned my language was "comme dandy," so he played the English toff who always finished his sentences with "*n'est-ce pas*." When I first met Severin I kept calling him "Savon" which Alex found very amusing, as it means soap in French. Both Alex and Francois began referring to him as Savon, and the new name stuck.

When I first shook hands with Alex I noticed that his fingers were just stumps. Although it did not seem to bother him or to greatly reduce his dexterity, both his hands had lost fingers at the first knuckle. When I saw that his feet were the same, I came to the conclusion that he must have suffered some horrific accident as a kid. I imagined him climbing up something which guillotined all his contact points. With hindsight, and given his love of adventure and the great outdoors, I think it was more likely to have been a severe case of frostbite. Never in the least self conscious about it, Alex was great with kids and used his hands to scare them in the daft monster games he often played and which they loved.

Our routine was to find a village school or church to stay at or camp in the bush if this was not possible. Staying in a village was always an opportunity to meet the elders from the school or church and usually we were greeted as if we were visiting dignitaries. We were given places to wash which was always a major pleasure after a day on the dusty roads. On one occasion, in an area which was particularly short of firewood, we were given three huge logs which were arranged in a star shape so that with a bit of kindling, we had a fire to cook on. When we had finished, the logs were extinguished and put away, ready for next time. Sometimes we were offered food which I found much more interesting than my usual fare of rice and sardines. My appetite was immense and invariably I ate much more than my companions, and on some occasions when the food was not easily recognisable, I would be the only one to eat it. Naturally Alex added this to his repertoire and I soon became the English toff who ate anything and everything that came across his path. They carried three spare tyres which to me was an extravagance, as they are very heavy, but when one went missing Alex suggested that "the English dandy" had eaten it.

Once we had crossed the border into Mali the roads became much more difficult as they were strewn with rocks the size of golf balls.

This meant that we had constantly to watch the road or take a tumble and so it was not possible to ride and look at the scenery. This was a pity because the terrain had become much more interesting and monkeys and baboons had begun to appear.

Our first target in Mali was the fairly large town of Kayes where the highest temperature in Africa was recorded a few years ago. It is a hot and humid town with a magnificent fruit and vegetable market. The people at the Catholic Mission were incredibly welcoming. We were given guest rooms, with electric fans and mosquito nets, and invited to eat with the Father. Although the house was not as opulent as the one where we had first met, the food was superbly cooked and the wine and whisky flowed. We washed and dried our clothes and the Father gave us the address of another mission on our route. Unfortunately on the day we left Francois, who had been feeling tired and listless, became so ill just a few miles out that all he could do was to lie prone by the side of the road. Fearing that it could be " le palu" (malaria) which was extremely prevalent in the area, we found a taxi to take him and his bike back to the mission. The taxi driver, aware that his passenger was very ill, demanded a premium payment which we paid with very bad grace.

By the time that we had cycled back to the mission, the Father had put Francois to bed and had summoned a local nurse. She was a very attractive young lady and while she examined Francois, we waited outside making the usual puerile jokes about Francois being the lucky one. When she emerged she confirmed the worst—that Francois had indeed contracted malaria.

Of all the diseases that travellers have to fear in Africa, I always felt that malaria was the worst, as it is the hardest to guard against. I had received inoculations protecting me from most of the major diseases like polio, yellow fever, hepatitis and cholera. To avoid bilharzia all I had to do was keep out of the water, and to avoid rabies all I had to do was avoid getting bitten by a dog (not always that easy on a bicycle, but possible). However, there is not much you can do to protect yourself against malaria apart from making sure you are not bitten by a mosquito, and that is not a realistic hope if you are cycling and camping in Africa.

Taking Larium once a week, I was protected to a degree from certain forms of malaria in that if I did contract the disease it would be less severe. As the mosquito parasite, which causes the problem, varies from region to region and is constantly mutating, there were also plenty of variations which I was vulnerable to, including a particularly nasty one which attacks the brain and was often fatal within 36 hours.

The Frenchman who was travelling in a Land Rover with the two French Canadian girls told me that Larium was an unnecessarily powerful drug whose side effects vastly outweighed the benefits it conferred. Some people can't take Larium because the side effects can be so severe. In my case they were not that bad but certainly significant. The first thing I noticed was that I started having the most extraordinary and vivid dreams. Not always unpleasant but certainly very odd. On a few occasions, memorably when playing cards, my eyesight became blurred. It is testament to my card playing skills that nobody in the card school noticed that I could not see my cards. The most unpleasant effect was that my skin became highly sensitive to the sun and refused to go brown. In my tent at night I would scratch myself to sleep and start again in the morning with lobster-red skin. The French government had recommended a milder drug called Savarine which the Frenchman felt I should switch to, and he offered me several months' supply which I declined. As I got farther south and deeper into malarial territory, a number of people I met went down with it and every one of them was French.

The hardcore travellers tended not to take any protective drug, partly because, like travel insurance, it contravenes the traveller ethic, and partly because they feel the best tactic is to keep alert to symptoms then seek local treatment. As the disease is so regionalised, it can be more effective to take the medicine that is given in the area you caught it and which is effective against the local strain. I have some sympathy with this approach but have also heard accounts of how bad it feels to get this disease, even when it is diagnosed and treated quickly. It is usually described as the worst experience ever suffered, and the residual damage is also quite extensive. Given that I was often on my own and a long way from medical help, I could not take the chance and so decided to stick with my Larium and all the colourful side effects that go with it.

The nurse asked if we had any Larium with which to treat Francois and told us to give him two tablets per day for four days. After the first day he started to feel better and we presumed he must have had a very mild dose. The following day we set off on a very basic, untarred road for Bamako. Francois was tired but seemed OK for the first few hours and then he started to feel the same symptoms as before. He was very pale and nauseous but for a reason that I did not understand, was refusing to take his second day's dose of Larium.

Fortunately we came across an elderly French couple in a very battered four by four parked at the side of the track. As Severin was debating what to do, I asked the couple if they were heading for Bamako and could they take Francois with them, as he was by now incapable of riding his bike. The Frenchman, who had lost his front tooth and so spoke with a lisp, pointed to a front wheel that was leaning at an alarming angle. The road was so bad that he wasn't confident the vehicle would reach Bamako but he was happy to take Francois. We strapped his bike to the roof, gave him some money and I gave him some Larium pills just in case he changed his mind about taking them. As we waved them off, Francois was looking very ill and I just hoped the car was stronger than it looked.

That night in the bush, both Severin and Alex were strangely upbeat and Alex even felt constrained to do a take off of Francois and his fear of snakes. As ever his act was very accurate but having seen the state of the lad when he left, I did not find it funny. Severin told me that Francois had always been a bit sickly, and suffered bouts of a depressive type of neurosis. They did not really think it was a good idea for him to fly to Dakar to join them. As he and Alex had ridden to Africa from France they had become acclimatised to the rigours of daily life but Francois had not had this chance and so they felt it had been inevitable that he would succumb to some ailment. I felt surprised, and even disappointed, that they were both being a bit hard on Francois. I asked why this was so and Severin explained that they had tried to dissuade Francois from coming and now, sure enough, he was giving them problems.

Alex had been in a manic mood ever since we had parted from Francois and by now he had built the fire into a bonfire and was dancing around it and leaping through the flames, whooping like a Red Indian.

A few days later the road quality had improved although it was still only a dirt track and we were covered in red dust and stones every time a vehicle went by. Coming towards us we saw the funny little four by four that had taken Francois, and the couple stopped to give us the news. Finding the hospital in Bamako had been difficult but eventually they had got him there, and they gave us directions. The man still had not had his tooth fixed and it was difficult for me to understand him. I gathered that the doctors had been unable to confirm that he had had malaria, as the Larium would have killed the parasites in his blood, but his problem was psychiatric rather than physical. He had behaved oddly in the car and was convinced there was a snake inside. I was pleased to see Alex looking very sheepish at this point. This couple had gone to a lot of effort on Francois' behalf and we thanked them profusely. The petrol money we offered was declined politely and they continued on their way. At least they had been able to get their wheel fixed in Bamako.

The road surface improved steadily and just before Bamako, became tarmac and we soon arrived at the city and found the local Catholic Mission. For a very small fee we were able to put up our tents in the grounds, provided we took them down again during the day so as not to make the place look untidy. Francois was in a hospital the other side of the city and we went to visit him. The building was modern and air-conditioned and the reception had a crisp, professional air about it. This impression was destroyed when the very unfriendly receptionist summoned a doctor who told us we could not see Francois, although he could not explain why. We said we would wait and settled down in the comfortable armchairs. About two hours later another doctor came to us and said, strangely, that Francois could see us in reception but we could not go to his room. As he shuffled in, wearing hospital garb, Francois seemed cheerful enough but his eyes were very heavy lidded and he seemed very sedated. As he recounted

his journey with the French couple he had to rouse himself from time
to time. Even in this state Francois made an effort to talk to me in
slower French and he said he was delighted to see me and thanked me
for coming. He confirmed what the French couple had told us—he
may or may not have had malaria but now the problem was of a
psychiatric nature.

Bamako, seen from its bridge over the Niger, is both beautiful and
ugly—a perfect example of an African city. The bridge's pedestrian
section is made from concrete planks about two inches too short.
Because they are too short, they wobble dangerously as you walk on
them. For this reason many of them are broken, further increasing the
risk of injury. As you walk across the bridge, you have to watch your
step so closely that it is not possible to appreciate the stunning vista
before you. If you stop you block the route for the hordes of other
pedestrians, all skipping from one block to the next. A beautiful river
crossing is ruined by the inexplicably missing two inches of concrete.
At the end of the day, the air by the river is appreciably cooler than the
air in the city. Unfortunately the river is also used as a giant open-air
toilet so that the overall effect is rather like a beautifully air-
conditioned gents' lavatory.

In this city, everyone is trying to make a buck and every inch of
pavement is taken up by somebody's livelihood, be it a workshop, a
stall or a rudimentary café. Walking across the city is therefore
difficult but fascinating, as there is always something to watch.
Women with just a few pots make a little stove and lay out a couple
of benches and then sell the most delicious food. Mixed spicy beans,
millet and milk with ice, are all very cheap but with a marginal pricing
policy that takes your breath away. Nothing is sold by the bag or
plate—even the chips are sold individually. On my last night with Alex
and Severin we decided to have a "grande bouffe" or celebratory
banquet. With Alex's brother who had met up with us in Bamako,
another French traveller, and a couple of girls from the Mission (one
of whom was to become responsible for Severin's first shave in
months) there were seven of us for dinner. Someone went for beer,
someone for meat and I was in charge of getting the chips. I found a

woman selling chips and I asked for enough for seven people. She asked me how many chips did each require and I guessed at ten. I waited while she patiently counted out seventy chips and packed them into a sheet of newspaper.

I visited Francois in the hospital three more times while I waited for my visa for Burkina Faso, and each time he appeared weaker and less coherent than the previous time.

Long after I had left Bamako, I met Alex and the clean-shaven Severin by chance on the road in a little Jeep. They were on their way to another SOS Village near the Dogon Country and we put my bike in the back and I joined them in the village for a couple of days. They told me that Francois' medical insurance company had arranged for a nurse to be flown from France to accompany him on the flight back. Nearly a month later he was still in a psychiatric unit near his hometown of Nantes.

Chapter 9

Back home, while I was preparing for my trip, someone suggested I should do the ride in aid of a charity. Not wanting to make formal plans or set myself targets, I was very reluctant at first. I also felt a bit awkward asking my friends for money—it was a bit like asking someone to sponsor my holiday. Eventually I decided to raise money for a charity because, on purely selfish grounds, it might be useful for me to have an organisation out there to call upon in times of need. In a similarly selfish vein, I also thought it would help deal with the question I knew I would get a lot: "Why are you doing this?" It is much easier to explain that you are riding a bike from Manchester to Cape Town for a charity than to give the truthful answer, which is that you don't really know. As it turned out, most Africans were just as perplexed with this answer and I was never really able to come up with an answer that satisfied them. Westerners had less difficulty accepting "raising money for charity" as a reason, although I tended to feel a bit of a fraud, as they assumed it was my main motivation which was not the case.

A trawl through the various charities on the Internet revealed that the Save the Children Fund was doing a lot of work in Africa, and the projects they were involved in seemed to me to be relevant. Their regional organiser, Chris Whitfield, was keen and helpful and he gave me the pledge forms which friends and colleagues quickly completed to raise nearly £4,000. Chris also gave me a list of SCF offices in some of the countries I was planning to cycle through. He was keen for me to visit them, as it would be an opportunity to get some publicity for the local projects. For me it was a bit of local security and maybe a chance to have a cup of tea and a chat.

One of the offices on the list was in Bamako, just round the corner from the Catholic Mission, and I telephoned to see if they would like me to pop round. A secretary put me through to a manager who seemed to be very suspicious of my motives but eventually agreed to a meeting—albeit three days hence. My preferred routine was to cycle all day, every day unless something prevented me, but I was curious to see what SCF was about and so decided to kick my heels for a couple of days.

The office was housed in an unremarkable building behind a big school and consisted of a general office and the manager's office. The secretary was suspicious to the point of unfriendliness and I had to wait nearly an hour to see the manager. He was a fresh-faced Malian in a western suit with a rather subdued manner. I explained to him how I had been given his address in the U.K. and that as a lot of people had sponsored me, I wanted to feed back to them what SCF were doing in Mali and thus how their money was being spent. In particular, I wanted to visit an actual project so I could see it at first hand. Once he had understood what I wanted, he relaxed visibly and his demeanour became more upbeat. Unfortunately, however, the office was soon to be closed due to lack of funding and so were the other two offices I had planned to visit in Ghana and Burkina Faso. This explained the less-than-enthusiastic welcome I had received but I still found it disappointing that there was no project to visit. Even more disconcertingly, I found it very difficult to pin down exactly what the Fund had been doing and I put this down to the manager's naturally low morale. After our meeting we walked back into the general office where he said something which I did not understand to the secretary which completely changed her attitude and she became almost gushing in her interest in my journey. Nonetheless as I rode away I felt that I had learnt very little—and I had not even been offered that cup of tea.

About a week later, as I was riding on my own towards Mopti, I was overtaken by a bright red Toyota which stopped in front of me and I was hailed by the same guy. He was on his way to a meeting in Mopti where he hoped to get some good news about funding. Understandably he was in a buoyant mood, as it seemed he was going to keep his job after all. We had a brief chat, which amounted to not much more than an invitation to admire his new car, and then he was on his way. All in all I felt the entire SCF encounter had been very unsatisfying. I suppose I had anticipated meeting a kindly old Albert Schweizer type dedicated to improving the lot of the poor little orphans in the area and I had got someone who, in appearance and outlook, could easily have passed for an estate agent or a stockbroker.

My couple of days with Alex and Severin at their SOS Village was more fruitful in that the objectives of the charity were clear to both understand and to see. The village took on very young children and looked after them in family units with "mothers" and, all importantly, saw them through school. Both my friends were highly enthusiastic about the work of the villages and loved being involved. Alex never tired of larking around with the kids, who adored him, while Severin tended to be a little more distant but was equally committed to their well being. The buildings were clean and modern and from what I saw of the food, they were probably among the best-fed kids in Mali. Severin told me, with some pride, that even the siblings of a child in care would be taken in and looked after. Some of the "kids" were clearly in their late teens or older and I was told they could stay as long as their education required and some even came back to help out with the younger ones.

The Father was a large jovial man who enjoyed lavish meals every evening and seemed to have an easy, affectionate relationship with all the staff, the "mothers" and the children. There were eighty children in the village, in family units of eight, and they all went to school and shared the chores in the village. They were healthy and happy and I felt a bit churlish when I asked Severin how they were selected from

BASIL JOHN MANDY

all the thousands of miserable, underfed kids you see trying to scratch a living on the streets of every African city. He didn't know, or wasn't saying, but thought that it is better to help a few than do nothing at all. I still don't know how they select the kids but as this was Africa, I suspect it is better not to know.

Whilst there are charitable works in evidence all over Africa, the only other one which I got to know was the Peace Corps. I met an American girl in a campsite near Accra, who had been in a Peace Corps' village in the Ivory Coast until the civil war had driven her out to Ghana. She told me a lot of the background to the war which I had previously not really understood, and from the standpoint of the rebels, as she had been working in the north—the rebel area. It was enlightening to listen to her very lucid account, as the only paper I had read gave the government angle only. Apparently, to secure a Peace Corps' place is the highest ambition of many American graduates but when I asked her what they actually did, she laughed as if I had caught her out. She said, "Yes, I see what you mean," but I had not meant anything. Eventually I gleaned that these young Americans did not have any particular skills to offer and that the prime objective was to enhance their CVs and the prime beneficiaries were themselves. It was just assumed that, being American, and educated, they would have something to offer. Their very presence would have the effect of improving the circumstances of the less fortunate African. In fact many of them spend a lot of money taking up one of these positions and I wonder if most Africans wouldn't prefer just to be given the cash instead.

It was only after this conversation that I began to question the effect that the Western charity industry was having on Africans. Nobody can doubt that charities have saved millions of lives over the years, and have eased the lot of millions more. It is too easy to knock charity projects on the grounds that they are short term, particularly as there is so much emphasis on sustainable development these days. Riding through Africa on a bicycle does not give you any special insights or answers, but it was clear to me that the continent is not only in a mess but that there are no obvious signs of progress. This lack of progress was probably my biggest disappointment in Africa and naturally I pondered this at length. I came to the conclusion that too many Africans, and sadly young Africans in particular, were in thrall to the perceived superiority of the West. Bluntly, it was as if they thought the white man is more intelligent than the black man. This is why he is more affluent than the black man and in turn this gives him the opportunity (and even the duty) to look after the black man. Each and every African problem has a clutch of white charities trying to solve it and I suspect this has led to the dependency culture, which was so in evidence in every country I visited.

Trying to understand why I had found myself agreeing with Marlies' observation about the superiority of the white man, I think it was this air of dependency that had influenced me most. After years of colonisation, then globalisation, the charities are reinforcing the sense of inferiority of blacks and the innate superiority of whites. Why else do Africans accept the preposterous and arrogant notion that a bunch of inexperienced Peace Corps youngsters, fresh out of college, can do something that they themselves can't?

The price that is paid for the good that charities do in Africa is the lowering of the self-esteem of African people. Whether it's famine, AIDS or desertification, the attitude to problems seems to be give them to the clever white men to sort out. They've got the money and they've got the brains. Look at any of the successful, strong cultures throughout history and you will see that their progress is underpinned by high degrees of personal independence and self-esteem, qualities that have been eroded in Africans over the years.

As I rode through the continent and pondered why so much of it is a mess, and not getting any better, one of the very few solid conclusions I came to was that the western charities should leave African problems to Africans. The essence of charity is that people are not equal. In fact all the agencies, governmental and non-governmental, and indeed anyone who is there because they think they can do things better than local people, should have the humility to question whether Africa might be better off in the long term if they just went home.

Tony Blair opined that Africa is a "stain on the conscience of the West" and came up with an "African Commission"—a forum to discuss the problems of Africa and devise solutions. Maybe this is a well-intentioned, genuine effort to help; maybe it is just spin. Its effect on African people can only be to reinforce the notion that the white man knows best. In the long run, efforts of this nature do more harm than good. For centuries Africans have had western notions of civilisation foisted upon them—democracy and Christianity being two of the most notable. Given how many people in the west are alienated by their own democratic process, and when you consider the farce that was the 2001 election in America, I wonder why democracy is seen as the holy grail for Africa. As for western religion, with its central tenet that we should be content with our lot, however miserable, you can see why it is popular with the ruling classes of whatever colour, but also that it never was and never will be a driver of progress. I thought of Jean, the hippy from Goree, and his analogy of Africans as trees, not inclined to move, and am forced to the view that excessive Christian religiosity doesn't help either. African societies worked fine before the advent of the white man, with social structures that developed differently but which perfectly suited their own environment. Destroying or denigrating these structures has done untold harm to Africa and to the African psyche.

However, of all the damage done to African people, it seems that today the most harm is done by the IMF and the World Bank. I had heard about the activities of these organisations before I left the UK but never properly appreciated the reality until I listened to Jean, and realised why Africans so often appear helpless.

In Ghana, I stayed at a campsite where I woke up in the night with very severe diarrhoea. The area had no running water and all the water in the site was carried in by road tanker. Unfortunately, that night the water had run out so I had nothing to put in my bucket to flush the toilet. To make matters much worse, I didn't make it to the toilet in time anyway. I desperately needed water and without going into too much detail, I was lucky that the campsite was on the beach and I was able to wash in the sea, by moonlight. The reason there was no water was that the IMF had insisted that all utilities in Ghana were privatised and since that time the water supply became a very hit or miss affair. Just outside Accra, I rode through a huge shantytown and stopped at a standpipe and asked if I could take some water. The local guys just laughed and said there had been no water in any of the standpipes in the area for years. Again, IMF enforced privatisation was the cause of the problem.

Originally, the IMF was designed to create stability and opportunity for underdeveloped countries. Today it is the means by which the neo conservatives in Washington apply influence to serve their own purposes and, tragically, while the IMF and World Bank lines the pockets of a minority, the people it really hurts are the very poor. Governments are forced to apply austerity measures and it is the poor who are denied schools, hospitals and decent housing. Farmers have to contend with high interest rates and appalling disadvantages in their attempts to trade with the West. If the West really wants to help in any meaningful way, they should just waive the crippling debts owed by African countries and then let them get on with running their own economies in their own way.

I only met one senior governmental official, a personal friend of an Indian family who had befriended me, and I have no idea how effective he was in his job. However, he was short and fat, arrogant and very conscious of his high status. The Indian family ran a successful local garage and no doubt he was a very useful connection. We were both invited to a superb Indian meal and, uniquely in Africa, I was out-eaten! I had no difficulty imagining that he conformed to the stereotype of the African politician and that he served the interests only of himself and his extended family. As I rode, I reflected that a lot of Africa is very poorly governed and that maybe it is charity, aid and Western intervention that keeps bad governments in power. If we left them alone, they could come up with a power structure that suited the African condition, and the alien structures with which we have saddled them could be allowed to whither and die in the hot African sun.

The night before the day of departure, packing for the journey.

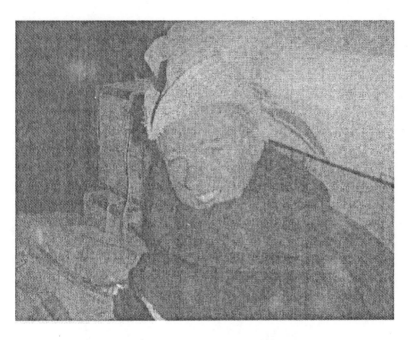

The train ride from hell—the wizened old man
unrecognized by his family.

The author with his perfect cycling partner, Massami.

In the tent of the nomadic family,
somewhere in the desert between Choum and Atar.

Campsite in the goat patch, Isle de Goree.

A village shop—locals gather round
whenever I stop for provisions.

The author with nineteen South African charity cyclists, one physiotherapist, two mechanics and a tour manager. A different way of cycling.

At the start of a gruelling mountain pass in Morocco.

Pius and family at the homestead in Swaziland.

A large black petulant thumb mars a photo in Ladysmith.

"Henke the Liar" drops us off at the end of his farm track.
My brother Steve is in the background.

St Louis, Senegal, New Year's Eve.

A typical Dogon village.

The coast of western Sahara is littered with wrecks—
but so far no trouble with the bike!

With my lovely Aunt Gerry, in Pietermaritzburg, South Africa.

Aunt Gerry.

Chapter 10

One of the effects of the growth in third-world tourism is that it is now virtually impossible to visit any place which people find of interest without being accosted by locals offering their services as a guide. In some areas, guides have to be suitably qualified and they are regulated by a local body. Their offering and their prices are controlled and have to conform to an agreed framework. Just because a guide is "official" doesn't necessarily mean that you will get what you pay for, but they are much more likely to deliver than the unregulated variety, the self-appointed guide. These are far more common and can be so insistent that some tourists will hire them just for a quiet life, or even just to protect themselves from the attentions of other guides.

In Ouagadougou, the capital of Burkina Faso, there is a typically African market—big, brash, full of colour and well worth a visit even if you don't want to buy anything. As I approached, a skinny, scruffy and rather shifty guy came up to me and asked if I wanted a guide. Feeling a bit irked that I was getting hassled so soon, I nonetheless managed a friendly smile as I declined his offer, explaining that I wanted to just wander round on my own for five minutes. As I was saying this I made a mental note to watch him, as he looked as if he had the flexibility and the skills to shift from guide to pickpocket, if the situation required.

In clothes that I had worn day and night for six months, I often managed to avoid the more tenacious sales pitches that confronted better-dressed tourists. Unfortunately this guy clung to me like a leech and nothing I could say would convince him that I did not want to give him my money. The market was truly fascinating in that it catered purely for local people but with this guy's grip on my elbow, I could not give it any attention. Eventually I became so exasperated that I broke a golden rule and rounded on him, cursing and swearing. He looked at me with a mixture of surprise and hurt as if wondering how a mere ten minutes of harassment could have led to such an uncivilised outburst. However, as a few bystanders were getting interested, he just melted away and disappeared into the crowd, just like any good pickpocket. Relieved to have got rid of him and particularly that the scene hadn't turned nasty, I made my way towards a stall selling a huge array of dates. Even before I got there, I felt another touch on my arm and the dreaded words, "*Voulez vous un guide, mon ami?*"

The prevailing advice about guides is to avoid them or to be very careful about engaging them: always agree precisely what is on offer and how much it will cost. There were only two occasions when I took a decision to use a guide and the first time was during my first day in Africa. At the border between Spanish Ceuta and Morocco, I was struck by how third world everyone looked. The contrast between affluent, fashion-conscious Ceuta and Africa proper was stark. Suddenly there were huge numbers of people on the road but a large proportion were on foot or on donkeys rather than in shiny cars and, typically in Africa, lots of people were just sitting around. However the defining icon of third-world Africa is the old lady carrying a ridiculously large load, either on her back or, farther south, on her head, and there were lots of these as I crossed into Morocco.

The dramatic culture shift excited and unnerved me in equal measure and I remembered the warnings I had been given about the touts and thieves all clamouring to relieve the innocent tourist of his money. In particular I had been told that if I changed money at the border, I would need to keep my wits about me or risk being ripped off. However, I needed to get some currency and as I pushed my bike through the border gates into the tumult, I had my antennae raised for offers. A young child shouted something at me but, assuming he was offering me drugs, his sister or himself, I ignored him. His shouts became more insistent and I saw that he was indicating that a policeman was calling me. Uncertainly I went back to the gate where the policeman wanted to know why I had "1974" etched on the back of my trainers. I said that was the year I was married, as if that explained it, and he smiled and asked how many children I had. I told him I had two and he asked if they were a girl and a boy. I confirmed that they were and he beamed and waved me on my way.

As I threaded my way through the crowd, I was disappointed to note that nobody was clamouring to change money for me and in fact I was being completely ignored. In a way, being ignored also made me feel relieved and as I set off for the first major town of Tetouen with the wind at my back, I felt a renewed confidence and sense of well being.

I still needed local currency and at the first village I pulled into a little café and explained to the fat, jovial waiter that I had no money but that I wanted a mint tea. He sat me down and brought me a glass, a little silver teapot stuffed with mint leaves and a plate of biscuits. As a cyclist, this was nothing short of heaven and I looked forward to riding through the country making regular stops for treats like this. Had I realised that the next day was the first day of Ramadam, with food and drink off the menu from sun up to sun down for a month, my high spirits might have taken a tumble.

Knowing that I was looking for a moneychanger, I expected my friendly waiter to summon up some shady relative to do a deal with me. Instead he gave me directions to the nearest bank where my travellers' cheques were changed without any fuss and at a very good exchange rate. When I got back I settled up and the waiter gave me an impromptu lesson on the coins and notes that make up the Moroccan currency. Roadside cafes are an important element of long distance cycling—as much for the opportunity to exchange a few friendly words as for whatever you might consume. In the previous country, Spain, I had got used to excellent coffee but not much else from the predominantly surly waiters. By contrast here I felt genuinely welcomed and my apprehensions about being alone in Africa lifted.

As I got near Tetouen, two guys on a smoky moped pulled alongside and the passenger shouted, "A thousand welcomes to my country!" His family ran a small hotel in the medina where I could stay for the "Moroccan price" of 30 dinars, about three euros, including shower. Being in such a sunny mood, I agreed to follow him and we passed through the rather drab modern town and into the narrow, twisty streets of the old quarter. In the bustle I lost him from time to time but thanks to the huge clouds spewing from the moped's exhaust I was able to track him into the heart of the medina. We stopped outside a tiny entrance to a dwelling with a hand-painted sign, Hotel Kati.

Inside, Abdul introduced me to a large smiling lady whom I took to be his mother. They conversed quickly in Arabic and Abdul told me the price was 50 rather than 30 dinars, a price I was happy to accept, as the place was clean and friendly. In the background there were two quite attractive girls who smiled shyly at me. Abdul was not in the least embarrassed by the price hike and with a big, gap-toothed grin informed me that I could put my things in my room and he would then give me a guided tour of the medina. Having had a glimpse of the medina, I realised that I would need a guide or I would get lost and I thought Abdul, being one of the family, would be a better bet than a total stranger. I asked him how much I would have to pay and he said he wasn't interested in money, only friendship and we could sort that little detail out later. The mother insisted that I put my bike in a little anteroom where she could lock it away from all the thieves who, apparently, were everywhere.

A little later I was trotting after Abdul as he set a fast pace through the teeming little nooks and crannies of the medina. Some of the streets were more like tunnels, as they were so narrow, and the activity within was intense. I would have loved to loiter, as it was my first experience of a medina and I found it stunning in its interest and variety. The atmosphere was exotic with sounds and smells that were totally new to me, but in such an alien environment I would have felt vulnerable had it not been for Abdul, forever gesticulating at me to keep up.

Before setting out I made sure that Abdul knew I did not want to make any purchases and he was very happy to agree that he would not set me up—after all he had no interest in money, only friendship. Our first port of call was, of course, a carpet shop. I was introduced to the owner, a big guy who looked like he took no nonsense. He shook my hand a bit too firmly, sat me down and offered me a mint tea. I explained that I was on a bike and couldn't buy a carpet, as I couldn't carry it. Not to worry, just have a look and enjoy the tea in friendship. An old guy appeared with a pile of carpets, which he proceeded to spread in front of me. I admired the carpets and finished my tea, which was delicious, and after a decent interval I stood up to leave. The owner stood in the doorway blocking my exit, looking even more hefty, and explained that even on a bike I could buy a carpet and have it sent home. He showed me a book of courier receipts of previous customers to prove that I would get what I paid for. With my confidence draining I told him that I was travelling right down to South Africa and was on a tight budget. He demanded to know how much was my budget and I told him the truth—six euros a day. Abdul was nowhere to be seen and the owner's demeanour was getting steadily less friendly. He told me that Abdul was a "good family man" and that he depended on the commission that he would earn on the sale of the carpet.

I reflected that on the way to the shop, Abdul had bragged about how he was doing "jiggy jig" with one of the girls at the hotel, but kept that to myself. Feeling a bit indignant, I said that I had budgeted for Abdul's time but that I had made it clear from the outset that I had no interest in buying a carpet. With a look of utter disgust he turned his back to me, so allowing a space for me to squeeze outside where a slightly sheepish Abdul was waiting for me. Once again we set off at a cracking pace, me telling Abdul I would not step inside any more shops, Abdul reassuring me that that was fine by him—no more shops.

Within five minutes we were inside an old apothecary and I was being introduced to the owner as if I was an old friend. My protestations were ignored and I was given more tea and a short discourse on the uses and sources of the various herbs and medicines in stock. I must admit it was fascinating and when he got to a potion for back pain my ears pricked up. I had strained my back in Spain and it was getting steadily worse, so I asked how much it was. We agreed a reasonable price and he offered me a free massage to go with it. Not wishing to push my luck I declined, as I had never had a massage and I was not too keen on letting this old geezer loose on my back. Naturally he ignored me and beckoned over a stunningly beautiful girl and told me she would do the massage. I asked where she would do it and he pointed at an upholstered bench at the back of the shop. She spent about 10 minutes working the oily potion into my back and when I stood up the ache had gone. I never again had a problem with my back and eventually I used the remaining oil on my cycle chain when it dried up in the desert.

Seeing that I was happy again, Abdul's cocky attitude returned and I asked him to take me to a good restaurant. We dived off again into the middle of the medina, which was becoming ever more beguiling. The restaurant he chose looked fairly ordinary from the outside but inside it was palatial, carpets on the walls and tables laid out as if in readiness for a banquet. The waiter was smartly dressed in traditional dress and he suggested I have the set meal. The only other punters were a large party of tourists who were so subdued that I could not even establish what country they were from. Their presence had the usual effect of draining the excitement from the situation but also of making me feel that I was less likely to have my throat cut or be sold into the white slave trade. Only when they all stood up to leave did I realise they were American but they did not acknowledge me and I never did find out why they had been so uncharacteristically quiet.

Abdul seemed oddly ill at ease and I ordered a set meal for him and told him I would pay for it. It was a magnificent meal of many courses with a fish tajine and couscous as the highlight, but Abdul only toyed with some courses and ignored others. As usual, my appetite was awesome and I saw off all of my meal and most of Abdul's. I could see he was astounded by how much I ate but it came as no surprise to me, as I was regularly eating vastly more than I did in my other life. During the meal I tried to get Abdul to give me some indication of how much he was planning to charge me but he would only reiterate that he had no interest in money, only friendship. When the bill came I was a bit shaken by the size of it and said to Abdul that I would not be able to afford to eat again for several days. He shrugged and said never mind, it was my first day in Morocco. He was right too, I had eaten a double banquet and had thoroughly enjoyed it. It was the day before Ramadam and, although I didn't know it then, I was to get plenty of opportunity to cut back on my food intake.

After coffee, Abdul insisted on taking me to a Berber market, as he claimed this was part of his "official" tour. I was beginning to find his bullshit rather amusing but I was also getting myself ready for the argument when we came to settle up. The market was no more exotic than any other part of the medina except that the stallholders were in the distinctive pointy hats favoured by the Berbers, and we left after no more than a cursory glance.

On the way back to the hotel, Abdul took me to the Place Hassan which he said marked the extent of how far I could safely venture into the medina on my own. For once he seemed totally sincere and I was quite touched by his concern. Back at the hotel he insisted on coming into my room and I felt that he also was expecting an argument. I took the opportunity to ask him where was the promised shower, as I already knew there wasn't one. Looking a bit disconcerted he opened and shut a few doors off the corridor and eventually said there wasn't a shower—but there was a toilet.

I realised that he was no more part of the family than I was, and I asked him how much he wanted for the guiding. He said two hundred dinars, about twenty euros. I reminded him that I had paid for the meal and offered him a hundred dinars. He reminded me that I had eaten nearly all his meal and said it had to be two hundred. Opening my bag of items I had brought for gifts, I offered him a Save the Children tee-shirt plus the hundred dinars. He saw that I also had some baseball caps and said that he would settle for one hundred and fifty plus a tee-shirt and a cap. I said no, one hundred plus shirt and cap. He was clearly getting desperate and said that for the extra fifty dinars I could have the jiggy jig girl, provided I supplied my own condom. We had passed the girl on our way to my room and Abdul had spoken a few words in Arabic to her and squeezed her arse. She had given me a particularly sweet smile. I told Abdul that I had given him my final offer but that I would throw in a ballpoint pen as well. He took a good look at the shirt and cap and agreed, saying that I needed to give him fifty for the room. I didn't fall for that one and insisted that we go downstairs where I could pay the lady of the house my rent direct. Once the negotiations were over we were best of buddies again and we parted on excellent terms, with Abdul reminding me that he had never been interested in money, only friendship. I felt that although he had tried his best to rip me off, he had provided reasonable value for money and he had given me something to smile about. I had no regrets about my encounter with Abdul.

Making the most of having a reasonably clean, cool room I bolted the door and lay down on the bed. I was woken a little later by a knock on the door and I opened it to find the jiggy jig girl with a packet of Kleenex in one hand and a jar of (I think) baby oil in the other. In a bit of a dither, I got the message across that I wasn't really up for it but would like to take her for a coffee in the morning. She didn't seem to be too disappointed but made me promise about the coffee. The next day was Ramadam and all the coffee houses were shut. I set off without being able to keep my promise.

The next time I agreed to take a guide was in Mali, shortly after I had left Wim and Marlies in a dust storm just outside Mopti, and this time I was left with anything but affectionate memories of the experience.

In Mali even the hardcore travellers spoke in glowing terms of the Dogon Country and I decided that it was an area which was well worth a visit, particularly as it has recently been recognised as a World Heritage Site. It consists of a series of mud-built villages ranged along a spectacular escarpment. The architecture of the villages is interestingly different but it is the history and belief system of the Dogon culture that is unique and truly fascinating.

Mopti is a river port near the Dogon Country and I had been told it was a good place to pick up a guide. However, I had been warned that faux guides were common and that I should be very careful in selecting someone. The guide had to be a true Dogon, as only Dogons were granted official guide status, and he should carry an identity card to confirm this. It was also essential to draw up a written contract with the guide which detailed exactly the terms of the agreement and the costs, and this should be signed by both parties. This all seemed a little excessive but I thought it would be as well to follow this advice.

In a dusty little campsite in Mopti I was approached by a good-looking and friendly guy called Babylon who said he was a guide and he was looking for a small group of people to take on a trip the following day. I said I was interested and he said we would meet later that evening with two other people who were interested. The others were a pony-tailed Frenchman who was obviously a hardcore traveller and therefore extremely reluctant to take on a guide, and a young Italian girl. It was pointed out to the Frenchman that everyone who visited Dogon Country had to engage a guide or else they would not be allowed access to the villages, something which other people had previously confirmed to me. The girl was a student on a gap year who said she had checked Babylon's reputation and that he was sound.

At the meeting, Babylon produced his guide's identity badge and then brought out a written contract that outlined in some detail exactly what he would provide. The tour on offer was either a two-day or three-day trek along the escarpment and included all meals, transport and accommodation. The Italian girl, Paola, was very keen and said that the quoted price was lower than average. The Frenchman was less keen, feeling that the price was higher than average and in any case he was "a free spirit" who resented being told that he needed a guide. *Pretentious sod*, I thought. He told Babylon that he would decide in the morning but Babylon needed both a signature on the contract and a deposit now or else all deals were off. The deal that I decided to strike was that I would sign up for one complete day and then maybe stay for the second day if I felt like it. Babylon wasn't terribly impressed with this but agreed, provided I paid the full cost of one day up front.

The reason why I had reservations about a longer tour was that each day's trekking took me further from Burkina Faso and so I would have to retrace my steps. There were no sealed roads in the area and the tracks were too sandy to ride a bike. Therefore I would have to push the bike from whichever village I ended up in to the village of Bankass where there was a rideable track. As a clincher to the deal, Babylon said that as he did not need to bring me back to Mopti, he would provide a donkey and cart to take me to Bankass from wherever I finished the trek. I signed, paid up and went to bed ready for an early start the next day.

In the morning a young sidekick of Babylon's came to me with a bag of Kola nuts which he told me I had to buy in order to give Dogon people as a sign of respect. Kola nuts are a local delicacy which supposedly deliver a lift in spirits when eaten. I found the taste so horribly bitter that I was happy to pass on the claimed spiritual uplift. The price the lad quoted me was so high that I couldn't even be bothered to haggle with him and I told him to clear off. He dropped immediately to half the price but he had irritated me and I walked off to a tirade of abuse and warnings of how I would offend the Dogons. As it transpired, I never saw anyone give a Dogon a Kola nut and in fact I never even saw a Kola nut in Dogon Country.

The Frenchman was packing up his things and he told me he had decided not to come with us. He was so hardcore that he didn't even use a tent but slept in a bag in the open, looking pretty cool but leaving himself at the mercy of mosquitoes and passing thieves. We chatted for an hour while I waited for Babylon to turn up in the promised Land Cruiser and I was struck by his laidback approach and complete lack of pretension, and I decided that I had misjudged him. A couple of days earlier he had lost his tent on a bus and now was caught between paying for a guide or buying a new tent. He was just as interested in my cycle ride as I was in his travels, which had taken him to every continent and taken up most of his adult life. As he slung his rucksack over his shoulder and trudged towards the road, I thought there are some hardcore travellers who are not doing it just for the badges. He was the genuine article and I was sorry he was not in the Dogon party.

Eventually Babylon turned up and to my surprise he was indeed in a smart new Land Cruiser, albeit two hours late. He blamed his late arrival on Paola keeping him waiting for the bathroom and I began to suspect that maybe she wasn't quite the disinterested neutral I had taken her for. Later, during the hour's drive to the Dogon Country she leant him a comb which he used with such nonchalance that I was forced to the uncomfortable conclusion that these two were an item. This was confirmed a little later when they shared a cigarette with comfortable familiarity.

In true African style, we waited for the car to fill up with other passengers before we could set off. The first stop was a filling station where Babylon asked me for petrol money. Disappointed that I seemed to have picked a guide who was always on the make, I pointed out that I had paid in full and that it was supposed to include transport costs. He shrugged his shoulders and walked off, muttering about the hassle of having to stow my bike on the roof of the car. His attitude to me had changed from the moment I paid over the money.

On the way we stopped at a small market town where Babylon had some unspecified business to attend to, and once again I was hanging around without really knowing why or for how long. I noticed that Babylon, who had an easy charm and appeared to be known and liked by everyone, was a bit of ladies' man. This fact did not escape Paola who was clearly annoyed by the excitement he seemed to generate in the local girls. She spoke fluent English and seemed to be feeling a bit guilty that she had knowingly misled me about her relationship with Babylon. She told me about her course at Milan University, African Studies, which I thought she was taking a bit too literally, and she plied me with questions about my own journey. When she had told me Babylon had a sound reputation, she had not let on that she was living with him. Getting ripped off by locals goes with the territory but I was seriously pissed off that a fellow European had had a hand in it, and I did not accept her olive branch. With more than a touch of malice, I reflected that when she got back to Milan the guys would not be too interested in a girl who had spent six months shacked up with a promiscuous African guy in AIDS-ridden sub-Saharan Africa.

We drove down the escarpment to the first Dogon village where Babylon organised a donkey and cart onto which were loaded our bags and my bike. I walked behind the cart as we made our way along the base of the escarpment on a very sandy track. The villages and the surroundings were almost completely cut off from the outside world—there were no electricity wires, no aerials and by all appearances the twenty-first century had not touched this area. We passed a man stripping a baobab tree of its bark and I wanted to ask why but my guide was a hundred yards behind, engrossed in a private conversation with his girl. I later learnt that the strips of bark were used as guttering on the mud dwellings.

All over Mali, I had seen postcards of Dogon villages and I had heard something about the amazing culture of the people, but to see them was one of the great experiences of my trip. Constructed entirely of mud, they had quaint little conical towers in which the grain was kept and the structure and geometry of each village was precisely in accordance with the centuries-old customs and beliefs. Behind each village, built into the base of the escarpment above the scree line, was a similar village, long abandoned. Interrupting the lovers' *tete a tete*, I asked Babylon why the people had moved down from the original villages and he told me it happened when Islam took over and people were instructed not to live higher than where they buried their dead. Knowing that there were Dogon villages also at the top of the escarpment, I asked how they managed to comply with this Islamist edict but Babylon decided I was just being clever and gave the usual shrug of the shoulders. I was very keen to visit one of the abandoned villages and I asked if he would take me up. He said the contract did not specify that he would personally do the guiding but he would get me someone else, and he wandered off. By this time I had decided that I would not extend my contract with Babylon, and when he turned up with a "guide" who looked not a day older than ten, I just smiled and followed him up the cliff.

My young guide was extremely agile and I struggled to keep up with him but when we got to the village he turned out to be enthusiastic and knowledgeable about Dogon history. He was able to answer all my questions in fairly clear French (which he learned at school) and even took me to meet an old holy man who lived alone in the abandoned village. He had a panoramic view of the plains below and apparently it was his job to keep watch for danger on behalf of the Dogons below.

Higher up and completely inaccessible, there were holes in the cliff face which were entrances to the homes of the Tellim people who lived there even before the Dogons arrived. I asked my guide how they got in and out. He told me the early Dogons believed they had wings, which did seem to be the only plausible explanation. Back in the village I thanked the lad and gave him a very handsome tip, which, I was pleased to see, he proudly showed a perplexed-looking Babylon.

All the larger Dogon villages have a visitors' house where the guides feed and accommodate their tourist charges, and while waiting there for lunch I met a group of young English travellers who also had engaged a guide in Mopti. Comparing notes, I discovered that their guide stayed with them at all times, answered all their questions with authority and charged a daily rate about half what Babylon was charging me. They were able to provide answers to most of the questions I had about the complex and fascinating Dogon culture. The reason why they had abandoned the villages was because when the area became desert, the water supply dried up and they had to move to the bottom of the cliff to dig wells. Nobody knew for certain how the "winged people" really accessed their homes but a theory was that pre-desertification, vines grew over the edge of the cliffs and these were used as access ropes.

Babylon turned up with a huge tureen of spaghetti and he, Paola and I sat down to lunch. The sauce was thin and watery and the pasta very overcooked but there was lots of it and as usual I ate enough to feed a small village. During the meal, Babylon told me more about Dogon culture, including the fact that they have a five-day week and their "day" finishes at six p.m. Their market day falls on the same day of their week which means that it always falls on a different day of the European week—very confusing for the tourists but indicative of how they have managed to conserve their old way of life.

After lunch our little party set off for the next village along the escarpment, where we were to spend the night. My bike was on the donkey cart behind which I walked and a hundred yards behind me came my "guide" and his squeeze. I was very reluctant to leave this charmed area but had decided that I did not want to pay to extend my trek when I was getting such poor value for money, and in any case I felt that I needed to get back to my journey. Whenever I wasn't "making progress" I found that I became restless. At a stop, I told Babylon that I would leave him after breakfast the next day and that I would take up his offer to transport my bike to Bankass. He said that was fine: I think he had picked up on my dissatisfaction with the level of service I was getting, but his next comment left me amazed at the sheer cheek of the man. He said that I would have to pay for my evening meal and for my night's accommodation. I reminded him that I had a signed contract in my pocket that specified that all my meals and accommodation for a whole day were included in the price which I had paid up front. As if he had anticipated my reaction, Babylon delivered his coup de grace with a flourish. Yes, he was responsible for providing meals and accommodation for a whole day, but we were in Dogon country and in Dogon Country a day ends at six p.m! My first reaction was that this was a joke that had perhaps gone down better with previous clients, but in fact he was absolutely serious.

In the end, Babylon did pay for these things but not before I told him that, come what may, I was going to eat and sleep at the next village and would not pay to do so. As a well-known guide, perhaps he wanted to avoid the embarrassment of a public dispute with a client, but I felt no satisfaction in winning the argument. I was just bitterly disappointed that this visit, which could have been incredible, had turned sour because I had chosen a greedy, lazy and stupid guide.

That evening I talked to Paola and told her that I could not understand how a person who was lucky enough to be born a Dogon, and so was eligible to be a guide in one of the few undiscovered places of interest in Africa, could treat his profession so casually and with such contempt. All he had to do was provide a decent service, build up a reputation for honesty, and he would have tourists beating a path to his door. Instead he allowed his instinctive desire to make a quick buck to take precedence over a golden opportunity to build a truly worthwhile and rewarding career. Paola readily agreed with all of this and even confided that she had tried to persuade Babylon to take a more farsighted approach with other punters in the past. Unfortunately I went too far in making a comment to the effect that it was just part of the "African mentality" and she got up and left me to my private indignation. Even though I was angry, my creeping racism was beginning to worry me.

No doubt I was feeling sorry for myself, but I was equally sorry for Babylon and all the poor, short-sighted fools like him who were never going to make anything of themselves because they couldn't rise above the grab-it-now instinct of the street hustler. This kind of approach is replicated in every society—witness our own cowboy builders and everyone else who would rather rip you off than build a reputation, but in Africa it is the norm rather than the exception. There is a tendency to eschew the long term in favour of the short term and, depressingly, this is a factor in the lack of progress that so disappointed me about Africa.

The next morning, Babylon told me there was no breakfast for me and even though he was, strictly speaking, obligated to provide it, I did not bother to argue. In any case Paola gave me five of the delicious Dogon bread loaves and these served as both breakfast and lunch. More of a problem was Babylon's declaration that he had never promised me transport to Bankass, as this meant I now had to push my bike through twenty-five kilometres of sand.

As I set off, Babylon, who was drinking coffee with Paola and a couple of friends, came over and asked if I knew the way. Feeling like a sulky kid, I said I would just follow the track and didn't need his help. He called over a grinning youngster and asked him to guide me. We were joined by more kids who insisted on pushing my bike. Babylon walked with us the first hundred yards and said he was sorry things had not gone well. I wondered if Paola had told him of my plans to write a book and if this was a belated attempt to improve his press. I decided I was just being cynical and we shook hands and parted almost like friends.

The kids pushed my bike enthusiastically until noon when the track became rideable. From time to time I saw groups of women with huge bundles on their heads walking in our direction. The kids told me they were taking their wares to the weekly market in Bankass. Watching their easy gait and happy demeanour as they went about just one of their weekly chores, I felt a bit small, and a bit more peevish than was justified.

I pulled myself together and later that day, at Ali's hotel, was lucky enough to bump into Marlies and Wim. They had also done a short trek in the Dogon Country, led by a guide whom they had met in Bandiagara, one of the Dogon villages. He was an old bloke who delivered all his promises and who had been recommended by other travellers. I vowed that in future I would seek out recommendations and then remembered that Babylon had been recommended. Unfortunately my source had not been the neutral third party I had taken her for. Still, we had a laugh over Babylon's classic sting of the "Dogon day" and the three of us spent the next week together cycling from Bankass to Ougagdougou.

That week was one of the happiest parts of my trip and also probably the one where the reality most closely matched what I had imagined when I first listened to Heinz back in the Paris street market. We cycled all day every day, camped in the bush and got our food and water in remote villages where we were greeted like royalty.

Wim was a lorry driver whose company allowed him to take extended leave whenever business was slow. He was a relaxed guy with such a thick mop of curly hair that he never had to bother with a sun hat. Marlies was a pretty woman with a wicked sense of humour but with a demeanour which suggested that she was too girly to cope with the rigours of this lifestyle. She put on make-up every morning and even rode in a skimpy little sundress. I expected trouble but could not have been more wrong. She was hard as nails and despite ongoing problems with her knees, I never saw her discouraged or unhappy. She only lost her serendipity when she was bugged by flies. When we arrived at a site to make camp the first thing she would do was to build a fire. My abiding memory of Marlies is of her sitting in the smoke (and thus protected from the "bloody flies"), fag in one hand, beer in the other, as serene as if she were on the balcony of a luxury hotel.

One particularly hot and dusty afternoon we came upon a small town with a brand new western-style hotel, about halfway between Bankass and "Wagga" (the locals' term for Ouagadougou.) There is an airport at Wagga and no doubt this was a stage post for the tourists who fly in to visit the Dogon Country. It was the only hotel in the region and we had a good nosey round, and to our delight we found it even boasted a bright blue swimming pool. It looked so inviting that we went in to see if we could use it for a few hours. The hotel and the pool were deserted but for some reason our request was turned down. Disconsolately we turned to troop out the foyer when Wim slipped the receptionist a few notes. Five minutes later we were doing bomb drops into the water. Naturally I had no swimming trunks but used one of my two pairs of underpants.

Wim had a video camera but used it so unobtrusively that I never felt bothered by it. He captured all sorts of images, vultures in a restaurant picking at our leftovers, a beetle digging a home in the soil, kids greeting us at a village well, Marlies sitting in the smoke of her fire. He promised to send me a copy and was as good as his word. When I eventually got home I played his tape and saw that he had also captured me fast asleep by the pool. Using his fancy zoom lens he had also got a great shot of my backside, exposed through two gaping holes in my skiddies.

We arrived in Ouagadougou in the middle of a film festival and the town was full of European buffs. Naturally Wim and Marlies were delighted and went off to one of the festival cinemas. Wandering back from a visit to a market, I was hailed from the interior of a street restaurant. It was yet another couple whom I had met earlier, at the campsite in St Louis, who had come to Ouagadougou for the festival. They were French and travelling in a smart white Toyota to Accra, Ghana, where they hoped to get a ship to transport them farther down the west coast of Africa. Their eventual destination was Cape Town and I wondered if I had met anyone who wasn't going there—would there be gridlock as we all filed into the city on our cycles, motorbikes,

Land Rovers and Toyotas? I joined them at their table and had a coke. They were full of the film festival and couldn't understand why I wasn't planning to see a film, particularly as I enjoyed French films and many of them were in French. At home I would have been mad keen but while I was on this trip, I found that I was always reluctant to get involved in anything that didn't have a direct bearing on my journey. They couldn't understand it, and now that I am back, I can't understand it either, although I could then.

The humidity in Ouagadougou was worse than anything I had experienced, and when we stood up all of us looked as if we had just crawled out of a swimming pool. As a final throw, they told me that all the cinemas were air-conditioned but still I resisted their blandishments.

That evening, Wim told me that he and Marlies would continue by bus because Marlies' knee was inflamed. I told him I had met a French couple who could maybe put their bikes on the roof of their Toyota and give them a lift. The guy had told me they were staying near the restaurant and Wim and I set off to find them. White Toyotas are not common and we soon found them, loading it up in preparation for departure the next morning. They were only too happy to take a couple of passengers and they made arrangements to meet the following day. To celebrate our last night, Wim, Marlies and I went to a restaurant that was billed as "traditional African" but which actually served Chinese food. It was delicious and we sat under a huge fan—bliss. Although Wim hardly ever drinks, Marlies and I managed to clean out the restaurant's stock of cold beer.

The next day, as I was eating my lunch of bread and bananas at the roadside, about 20 miles south of Ouagadougou and just north of the Ghana border, a white Toyota with two bikes strapped on the top pulled up. Climbing out the back, Wim put his finger to his lips, as curled up on the luggage was Marlies, sound asleep.

The next time I saw them was a fortnight or so later at a beachside campsite just outside Accra. They had heard that the "Englishman on a bike" was there and had found me. Marlies had had her hair plaited African style and looked fantastic. They were going to fly home the next day and so were ready to spend the afternoon on the beach drinking beer and cokes and reminiscing. But I had the beginnings of the runs—a bug whose effects were due to climax later that night.

We had been through a lot together and my spirits had been lifted immeasurably by their confidence and enthusiasm, but that afternoon I felt that I let them down. I turned down their invitation to spend the final night of their trip with them back at their campsite, mainly because I felt sick but also because I didn't trust my bowels to behave as we walked to their site. As we said our final goodbyes, I sensed that they were both a little surprised and disappointed that I had allowed a little tummy bug to get in the way of the party that the occasion demanded.

Chapter 11

I often get asked what I would do differently if I ever did it all again. The first point I make in answering is that I will never do it again or anything like it. Apart from the fact that I could not expect my employers to hold my job for another period of long-term leave, I doubt that my family would feel as positive and supportive about a second adventure of this nature. But what really makes it a non-starter is the fact that I just don't want to do it again. A lot of the hardcore travellers I met were clearly aghast that I planned to go back to my old life. For them, work was only a means to get together the money that allowed them to continue their travels, and they were proud of their addiction to travel. My first Monday back at work would be "The Monday from Hell"; all I would want would be to get back on the road.

In fact, the day I went home was one of the happiest days of my life and going back to work was a breeze. As the cliché goes, you only really appreciate what you've got when you no longer have it and after a long period without it, I now really appreciate my life in the UK. Apart from being with family and friends, I like not having to take anti-malaria drugs, I like wearing clothes that are not the ones I slept in and wore the day before, and the day before that. Water comes out of the tap and never needs to be purified. We have good beer, TV and football. However, the one feature of life, which I now appreciate as never before, is the feeling of security that we have in European countries. Of course there is crime everywhere and anyone can be a victim at any time. The difference is that in most African countries you are on your own whereas here you have invisible guardians with whom anyone who wants to take what is yours will have to contend. It is not just that we have police who are mainly straight and a judiciary that normally gets it more or less right. We have a society that is predominantly decent and not disposed towards crime.

Several years ago I was mugged while taking a short cut through a dark alley on my way home from work. My two attackers didn't manage to get anything from me but I got a broken nose and a sore knee where they had pulled me from my bike. A local householder came to my assistance and called the police who arrived in five minutes. They took a statement and drove me home, my bike in the back of their van. One of the officers made a comment, which touched a chord with me, "If these two guys carry on with their criminal lifestyle, they will be caught and they will end up in prison." Justice will be served eventually, and that made me feel better. The next day I got a call from Victim Support who asked me if I needed counselling after my ordeal. I didn't, and I never found out if my assailants were caught, but the point is I never felt that it was me, alone, against them. There were too many others on my side including, crucially, a member of the public.

I never really felt conscious of this sense of security until I returned from Africa, and my appreciation of it has never left me. By contrast, in many parts of Africa the police are so corrupt that people would not dream of intentionally getting involved with them, but it is not just that which makes you feel you are on your own. In South Africa, in a small white-owned grocery store, the owner told me as I paid for my items that I should not have left my bike outside. His wife had had to stand watch over it as I made my purchases. I pointed out that it was locked but he said, "Listen, there is always a man sitting in the shadows…he's not necessarily a thief but he has nothing. He sees your bike…he wants it…he takes it. That's how it is." Unlike so many white South Africans, he was not at all judgmental in saying this. You don't have to be a bad man to steal, if you have nothing (a concept we find hard to grasp in Europe), you will steal.

People in Africa have nothing to lose, they may even have AIDS, they may have a hatred of white people—and a rich white man passing through on a bicycle is probably fair game. The ancient tribal structures had strongly developed processes to deal with right and wrong but many of these have been broken down. In short you cannot rely on their social groups to act as a break on criminal activity in the way that we do in our relatively affluent and healthy society. In Africa, you are on your own, and if someone wants to steal your bike, it is you against him.

To help overcome the security issue, if I did do it again, the first thing I would do differently is that I would not go alone. I started my journey with a friend who rode with me to Lille and I was lucky enough to meet up with other cyclists on three occasions where we rode together for significant distances. In addition, my brother Steve, who lives in Durban, decided on impulse to borrow a bike and accompany me on the last leg to Cape Town. Without a doubt, these were the safest parts of my trip and I would always place more value on companionship and security than on the independence you have when alone.

Even without my diary, which I lost when I was robbed in Mozambique, I can clearly remember the times I spent with other people. The time I spent on my own, principally travelling through Ghana, Tanzania and Malawi, has become hazy and disjointed. A guy called Karl who was travelling alone on a motorbike called Mavis once told me that he had spent several hours in Angola watching some ants. He noticed that they appeared to have only two speeds, fast and stop. There was nothing in between. I asked him how long he had been on his own when he made this observation and he told me about a week. Karl was a strong, independent type and seemed to value experiences of this nature as much as the more obviously enjoyable aspects of long-distance travel. Being an introvert, I had thought I could handle being alone but I found that I became depressed and conscious of my loneliness after more than three or four days. Watching ants is no substitute for conversation, and long before getting engrossed in whether they really do walk at a constant speed, (and why), I would be fretting about them getting into my food or, worse still, into my tent.

Apart from helping to maintain your spirits, or in Karl's case, your sanity, a companion has other major advantages. The obvious one is that you feel more secure and so you can give more attention to the country you are in. You see more and when you come across local people you focus more on them and less on whether they represent a threat. The countries I engaged with the least were those in Southern Africa where I was both on my own and felt at my most vulnerable. You don't make friends while you're wondering if the person you have just met is about to attack you.

At an isolated but predominantly white roadside café in Mozambique, I was asked what I thought, at the time, was perhaps the most banal question put to me in Africa. It was lunchtime on a particularly rainy Sunday and I found myself in conversation with several tables of families who seemed to be out for their weekly treat. Most of them were South African, civil engineers trying to repair the damage caused by a severe flood, or on their way to a holiday destination on the coast. Outside was the usual array of big, flashy four by fours, mainly Toyota Land Cruisers. There was also one family who had lost their tobacco farm in Zimbabwe and was now farming in Mozambique. They had borrowed heavily to get started but things were looking up for them, and they were producing tobacco that they reckoned was even better than what they harvested in Zimbabwe.

Gradually, my story came out as all the tables took turns to quiz me about my journey. Just as I was getting ready to go, the tobacco farmer's wife, who had not spoken so far, asked me if I could expect to learn anything about a country just by cycling through it. In her view, I had done nothing more than scratch the surface. This was the first time anyone had made disparaging remarks about my odyssey and I felt piqued. I considered the sturdy vehicles outside, probably washed and maintained by servants, and thought, *How much do you learn in your air-conditioned, chauffeur-driven Toyota with all the doors locked?*

One of the benefits of riding a bike for any distance is that you think deeply about everything you see and hear—it is almost unavoidable. As I rode through the beautiful Mozambican countryside that afternoon, I thought about what that woman had said, and gradually I realised that she had hit upon something else that I would change if I did it again. She was talking about the fact that my routine involved spending each night in a different place. Not that far from the previous night, only a day's bike ride away, but different nonetheless. Naturally, I got to know the terrain really well, but in my whole trip I never really got to know a local person well. By the time I had allayed my initial suspicions, and established my own friendly intent, I was on my way again. The only people I got to know well were fellow travellers. If I did it again, I would make sure that I stayed in one place for long enough to scratch the surface a little deeper. It was not such a banal observation after all, and of course the Chinese have the appropriate proverb, "Men cannot see a reflection in running water—only still water."

Another thing I would do differently is that I would give some attention to the time of year when I would be in various parts of the world. I set off in September because that was when it suited my company for me to start and as Africa is either hot and wet or hot and dry all year round, it mattered not a jot when I got there. In any case I had no idea how long the various parts of my journey were going to take, so there didn't seem much point in detailed planning. As a result I traversed Morocco during the worst month of the year, the month of Ramadam, crossed Europe with wind and rain blowing into my face and finished my journey during the only truly unpleasant season in South Africa.

Ramadam is the month when Muslims do not eat, drink, smoke or have sex from sun up to sun down. Only the first two of these had much impact on my lifestyle, but given that I was on a bike, the impact was significant. Any other time, I would have stopped at least once an hour at the little roadside cafes to enjoy the sweet mint tea and little biscuits that are just ideal fuel for cycling. Almost as important, stopping at remote little places allows you the opportunity to break the ice with the locals, which has a huge positive impact on your morale and confidence while travelling through areas which otherwise appear strange and even threatening—especially when the kids are chucking rocks at you. As a bonus you can make a bit of progress in your French conversational skills.

Although I was sorry to miss out on all this, the main problem with Ramadam is that it does not apply just to good Muslims; it is considered impolite for anyone to eat or drink in public. During the first morning of Ramadam I saw a British couple harangued by a group of youths for eating in the street and I thought a lot of the vitriol was down to our leader's support for the war in Iraq. I vowed to take Ramadam seriously. A cyclist spends his life in public and I soon found that in Morocco you are very rarely completely on your own. Even in the remotest mountains the roads are never deserted—there are always people walking or just sitting watching the world go by. Many times I found the ideal spot to answer nature's call when somebody would suddenly appear or an unseen voice would hiss an offer of kif, the high quality hashish on sale everywhere in the Rif mountains. The lack of privacy was quite disconcerting.

Abstaining from food and drink was out of the question for me so I had to devise ways of fuelling up surreptitiously and quickly. I needed something I could keep in my pocket and sneak into my mouth, and the ubiquitous dates were perfect. Unfortunately, on the day I got caught out, the dates in my pockets were the sticky, sugar-coated variety. They are delicious but have the consistency of toffee and take a lot more chewing than the plain ones.

Instead of being a pleasant and welcoming interlude, cafes during Ramadam are full of hungry, thirsty, nicotine-starved, irritable men with nothing to do. They are places to avoid during the day, and even at night you have to wait until every Muslim mouth has been satisfied before any waiter will even consider serving the infidel, who has probably been cheating during the day anyway. One morning I made the mistake of stopping within sight of just such a café to sneak a handful of sticky dates into my mouth. A hawk-eyed Arab in traditional dress left the café and came striding towards me. To avoid the inevitable rollicking I tried to munch the dates as quickly as possible and just as he launched into his tirade I felt a tooth break under the strain. Sorely tempted to tell my aggressor to sod off, I nonetheless managed to mumble my usual apologies as I climbed on my bike to go off and inspect the damage. To my dismay, I confirmed that I needed a dentist and to further lower my spirits the weather took a sharp turn for the worse. Sale Rabat was the nearest town, about twenty miles away, and I decided to get there, find a campsite and then go find a dentist.

The sky had turned ominously black and the wind was getting up as I got to the almost deserted campsite by the beach. It was inside four concrete walls so that the view was restricted to the corrugated iron roofs of the surrounding houses, some of them clanging noisily in the freshening wind. It had the air of a prison compound. Eventually I found a small patch of grass which was relatively free of dog shit and broken glass, and with some difficulty I managed to erect my tent. The guy in charge of the site gave me directions to a dentist and I followed them carefully. I knew I was at the right place because there was a picture over the door of a tooth being yanked from a gaping mouth with a piece of string. To complete the image there was a glob of bright red blood spurting from the wound. I decided to look somewhere else, and with a stroke of luck I came upon a series of roads full of doctors' surgeries, chemists and modern-looking dental offices. I chose the smartest-looking one and entered a well-appointed reception area. The receptionist was sympathetic and arranged an appointment for two hours hence and I agreed to come back. As I was about to leave, the heavens opened and I asked her if I could wait in the waiting room. She said fine and even suggested I bring my bike into their basement, out of the rain. I sank into the most comfortable sofa in the world and two hours later I was woken from a deep slumber by a smart-looking lady in a white coat. Using a laser beam to check my tooth, which really impressed me, she told me I had broken a tiny filling and she could fix it without bothering with an anaesthetic. True to her word, it didn't hurt a bit and ten minutes later I counted out the forty euros she charged me. With the same sense of satisfaction that I got whenever I had my bike fixed, I left the comfort and tranquillity of the surgery and headed into the tempest which was raging outside.

Back at the campsite I was relieved to see my tent still standing and I crawled inside, took off my soaking clothes, carefully ate my remaining dates and went to sleep.

Just before dawn I woke up feeling shivery and sick, and very reluctantly I left my tent to spend the next half-hour in the filthy, freezing toilet block. When I got back into my sleeping bag, sweating profusely, I lay on my back watching the sides of my tent billowing in the wind. During the particularly violent gusts the tent would flatten against my face and I prayed that the loose sheets of corrugated iron on the neighbouring houses were not flying about overhead.

In the morning I was feeling too sick to cycle and the wind was still blowing its tits off so I decided to spend the day in my tent. But I needed to move it to the shelter of one of the prison walls, so with a huge effort of will I started pulling out the pegs. When I had finally got it down I sat on it with my head in my hands as I recovered my strength. The only other camper, a Frenchman with a trailer van, came over and, rather bizarrely, asked me how old I was. The rain was starting to fall again and I willed him to suggest that I put my bike in the back of his van and then drive me back to the UK. Instead he offered his hand, said I was a "very brave man," and walked back to his wonderfully warm, comfortable van and drove off.

All alone I remained perched on my rolled up tent with the rain falling lightly on my head, and then moved over to the wall. Even in the lee of the wall, the wind was so strong that I just could not put up the tent. It was all I could do to hang onto it as it billowed above my head like a giant kite. The poles were hideously bent and I had to give up; I went over to the reception hut to ask if there was a cheap hotel nearby. The guy said no, not in Sale, and pointed out that he had nice rooms on the campsite. I asked to have a look and we walked over the desolate site to a row of rooms which looked just like the cells of a Mexican prison. Each bare concrete cell had a plastic mattress on the floor and a high, barred window, nothing else. I needed somewhere warm and clean to sweat out my fever and the thought of spending even one night in that concrete box just appalled me. Without making any effort to be polite I declined the room and paid up for the night on the site. I remember feeling a bit surprised that the guy was put out that I didn't jump at the offer of his nice room. Battling the swirling wind which was throwing up swarms of black plastic bags and the occasional shower of sand, I searched but could not find anything resembling a hotel. Eventually an old man stopped me and said he had seen me twice and what was I doing? The tone of his question made me feel like a spy who has been caught out, and I blurted out that I was just a tourist looking for a hotel. He seemed not to buy my story but confirmed that there was no hotel in Sale and that I would have to cross the river into Rabat to get one. The bridge was long and I nearly got blown off it before I found a large crumbling hotel in Rabat overlooking a graveyard, which I thought might be handy. My room even had its own shower although to my great disappointment the water was cold. I spent the next two days in bed and by the time my fever broke, the windows and walls were running with sweat like an old cheese sandwich.

As I set off once again, heading south to Marrekesh, I wondered if my misfortunes were anything to do with Allah getting his own back on me for disobeying the Ramadam rules. Whatever, I made life difficult for myself and made a mental note that in a future life, I would avoid Morocco during Ramadam. Looking back on the experience as a whole, I see now that what I really missed was a bit of friendly support from the locals, which would have made all the difference. Unfortunately I could not be expected to legislate for having a leader who decides to align himself with an illegal American "President" bent on war.

Chapter 12

At a Decathlon store in France, I was told that my bike would probably not make it to the Spanish border, let alone to Africa. It was too cheap and too old. In fact, I was south of the Sahara before I had to even fix a puncture and apart from an occasional broken spoke, I was within striking distance of South Africa before I experienced any significant mechanical problems. In Mozambique, just north of Maxixe, my chain started to slip badly, as both it and the rear cassette were worn out.

To replace parts of this nature, I needed a well-stocked cycle shop and I decided that the most likely place to find one was Inhambane. On the map, Inhambane appeared to be the biggest town in the area and I had also heard that it was particularly beautiful with some great beach-side campsites. As I pulled into Maxixe, which looked a dump, I spotted a little ferry about to set off across the estuary to Inhambane, paid my fare and climbed aboard, wondering where they could possibly find space for the bike. The "conductor," a twelve-year-old lad with a very confident swagger, hoisted the bike nonchalantly onto the roof. We docked at a rickety pier half an hour later and I headed for the centre of town where I hoped to find a bike shop. There were lots of attractive old Portuguese colonial buildings to admire and the view back across the Bay of Inhambane was fantastic.

Amongst a crowd of smartly uniformed pupils on their way to school, I noticed a tall, shambling white guy with a beret exchanging banter with some of the kids. I crossed the road to ask him if he knew of a bike shop. He had the weathered face and world-weary air of an old sea dog and it transpired that he had spent most of his life in the Greek Merchant Navy. Without such a pronounced stoop, he would have been well over six feet. Typically, his first gesture was to put a huge mitt on my shoulder and ask me if I had a problem with my bike. I told him I just needed to replace some parts and he said he knew some people in town who could help me. Despite his laidback appearance he walked at a brisk pace and I struggled to keep up with him. As we walked, he greeted everyone with a flourish but was particularly effusive with females. The first shop he took me to looked more like a hardware store than a bike shop and the owner informed me that the only bike shop in the area was across the estuary in Maxixe. However, "because I was a friend of Nico's," he asked his young assistant to take me to a guy who ran a bicycle stall at a local market just outside the town centre. Nico told the assistant to bring me back to a café where we would have a late breakfast after I had got my bike fixed.

The assistant was a garrulous and enthusiastic lad called Enrico who loved England to such an extent that he wanted to ride back home with me. His English was very rudimentary but I managed to explain that I was going to South Africa first. I gave him my email address and he said he would contact me if ever he was able to fulfil his dream of getting to England. When we got to the market we made our way to the bike stall but to my disappointment we found it all locked up. It was the only empty spot in a sea of activity, and a trader told us the owner was having a day off and would probably be back the next day.

Enrico seemed to feel that he had failed me but I shrugged it off and told him I would just come back tomorrow. As we neared the café in the Central Market where I was to meet Nico, I offered Enrico a fairly sizeable tip, as I was grateful for his trouble, but he waved it away saying I was his friend and soon we would meet again in England. I hope we do but am not holding my breath.

Nico was tucking into a plate of fried eggs, and although it was mid morning, he and everyone else at the table had a huge bottle of beer. He called over the waitress and, with his arm around her rump, he ordered me the same.

Over breakfast, Nico told me about his life as a seaman and how he eventually came to settle in Inhambane, the most beautiful town he had ever seen with the friendliest people, about twelve years previously. He met and married a local girl, Maria, and together they set up a food stall and bar called the Black and White, in recognition of their coupling. The bar did very well for a few years and they lived in a smart new house with a servant girl and a gardener. Life was good until Boris, a German, showed up and started an affair with Maria, who won a messy divorce from Nico.

Telling me this, Nico was well into his third beer and his eyes began to well up. He was probably the most lachrymose man I have ever met, particularly when drinking which was a lot of the time. Everyone else seemed well used to this feature of Nico's and I was the only person who felt a bit embarrassed.

Boris and Maria took over the smart new house in return for an undertaking to pay the rent on Nico's current lodging but what really hurt Nico was that they also took his beloved Black and White. Everyone in town felt that Maria had acted shamelessly in robbing Nico of his pride and joy but the truly evil villain of the piece was Boris, not only an incomer but a German to boot.

Without Nico, the bar lost customers and began to lose money and soon Boris and Maria sold it to set up a taxi company. This prospered because they were both so obsessed with making money that they worked like slaves, and now more than half the taxis in Inhambane were controlled by MB Taxis. They even had a fourteen-seat minibus. So, with the ill-gotten gains they had screwed out of Nico, Maria and Boris had become fabulously rich but were completely friendless because everyone knew where their money had come from.

Crying freely as he told his tale, Nico soon cheered up as we talked of other things and he seemed to be genuine when he said he was happy with his friends who loved him even though he had nothing. Looking at the guys around the table, who seemed to be fairly prosperous businessmen with confident demeanours, I wondered if they loved Nico as much as he thought they did. They indulged him and laughed at his jokes but every now and then I thought I saw a knowing look pass between them. I decided that they certainly did not share Nico's contempt for Maria's business acumen or her work ethic. As we got up, I offered to pay Nico's and my bill but the guys just laughed and waved us away.

I explained to Nico that I was going to wait for the bike stall to open the next day and he promptly invited me to stay at his place. Although he had only one room, there was a veranda where I was welcome to put up my tent. The nearest campsite was at a local beach about six miles away and with my bike out of commission, Nico's offer was an attractive proposition. Besides, I enjoyed the company of this colourful loser and having been on my own since the trauma in Zimbabwe, I quite fancied the prospect of a night on the piss.

Walking to his house, which was in the middle of a poor residential area with sandy alleys between the dwellings, Nico told me that he had once put up a German couple who were hitching through Mozambique. Even though he had done this purely out of friendship, in the morning they accused him of having stolen their money. He felt this was typical of Germans, and he assured me that he had not stolen from them, but I wondered why he had told me the story.

Nico's house was brick built but his immediate neighbours were shanties, albeit neat and tidy. It was a single storey with two rooms, one of which was his and the other was let to a young black priest who clearly disapproved of Nico's bohemian lifestyle, but to his credit, tried to keep this to himself. Adjoining his room, Nico had a small shower cubicle, cold water only, which I used with great pleasure. Maria paid the rent and also for a maid, Esther, who Nico had to cajole into saying hello to me. I wasn't sure if she was just shy or very put out by my unforeseen presence: she had the air of a disgruntled wife rather than a maid. She was young and pretty and no doubt did more than just wash his socks. She made us coffee after coffee which we drank with rum on the veranda.

Nico was extremely widely read and had a view on everything from cookery to philosophy to African politics. As a pacifist, he was totally opposed to the American and British intervention in Iraq, and railed against the trickery that Bush had employed to get himself elected as president. I had already seen him speaking fluent Portuguese but he also spoke most of the European languages and was currently teaching himself Chinese. With the aid of a battered atlas he asked me to trace out my journey through Africa and he spoke with authority and warmth on most of the countries on my route.

Around mid afternoon, Esther turned up with an enormous tureen of spaghetti in sauce which she laid on the table. Nico asked me if I wanted wine and I said yes. He pointed at a little building where I could buy wine and told me to buy a certain type. I went to the shop and asked the old lady for two bottles of the wine and was given two cartons of the cheapest white Portuguese wine in the shop. It was perfect with the spaghetti.

After lunch, Nico said he wanted to show me the Black and White and I was keen to see it, as it clearly occupied a huge place in his heart. We walked back along the sandy alleys and across a school football pitch where some kids were playing. The ball came bouncing our way and Nico flicked it with his foot and juggled it before booting it back to the admiring youngsters. The alcohol had hardly affected him, although I was feeling a bit mellow to say the least.

On the way we were hailed by a group of guys at a street side bar, similar to the bunch we had breakfasted with, and I was introduced to each in turn. They all had the same affectionate regard for Nico coupled with the same barely discernible contempt for a loser, which I thought I had spotted amongst our breakfast companions. The drink of choice of the group was, rather surprisingly, gin and tonic and we both joined in. There was a large coconut tree nearby and I was told that a guy standing under it had recently been killed by a falling coconut. Apparently this was a common problem in the area. Eventually we prised ourselves away and once again my offer to pay for the drinks was met with a laughing refusal.

The Black and White was situated just off the road with the panoramic view of the estuary which I had admired earlier in the day, and it was much more than the basic street stall which I had been expecting. The bar consisted of a steel container with a hole neatly cut out of one side. This was surrounded by a concrete terrace under a canvas awning all held together by a very sturdy wooden structure. The whole affair was painted in black and white squares and it looked friendly and inviting.

The small knot of guys at the bar welcomed Nico warmly and he ordered a bottle of gin and some tonic which we carried to a table under the awning. A roly-poly guy with a permanent grin detached himself from the group at the bar and came to sit with us. This was Peace who was a particular friend of Nico's and lived a few miles away in a house he had built near the beach. He and Nico planned to construct a fishing boat and make a living selling their catch in the market. From his coat pocket, Nico pulled out a large piece of paper with the drawings and elevations of the craft, and the pair of them discussed modifications and made minor changes to the drawings. They both knew what they were talking about and I made a mental note to give them my compass, rather like a bottom drawer gift to the happy couple.

Just to the side of the terrace was a large, bare concrete square with an unfinished look and I asked Nico what it was. Unfortunately this was a sensitive issue and Nico's eyes began to fill as he told me of his plan to construct a giant chessboard where the punters could play with metre high pieces. Maria had been lukewarm about the idea, as it wasn't an obvious income generator, whereas for Nico, a keen chess player, it would have been a little piece of paradise. I could just see him holding court as he spent his afternoons beating all comers surrounded by his admirers with a never-ending supply of drinks. It was not to be, because Maria cheated him out of the bar before he could even paint the board's black and white squares.

Even without the chessboard, I thought the Black and White was a lovely spot and, perhaps a little carelessly, I said as much to Nico and the floodgates opened again.

By now I was as comfortable as everyone else with Nico's tears and Peace and I chatted at length. He had an open, amiable face but it was clear that he was far more of a realist than Nico and I thought their partnership could well succeed with someone to put some drive behind Nico's dreams and schemes. During the evening people joined us and left us and, without exception, they were effusive in their greetings and regard for Nico. I tried hard to pay for some drinks but always without success. Nico never even tried.

Peace invited us both to his house on the beach the next day. He was going to slaughter a pig and he wanted us as guests of honour, and to stay the night. I was really keen to get my bike fixed and get underway, but I enjoyed the company of both these guys and in any case was intrigued to see Peace's house. I accepted with gratitude and the three of us parted amongst elaborate handshake rituals and much appreciation of the good fortune we all had in making each others' acquaintance.

That night, as we finished off his rum on the veranda, Nico talked until the small hours about his life in the Merchant Navy. He had a wealth of lurid "sailor" stories featuring the usual drunken shore leaves, brothels and fights but he had also taken the opportunity, given him by long hours at sea, to pursue his interest in politics, literature, languages and, dearest of all to his heart, philosophy. He spoke passionately about philosophy, and every so often would plunge into his room to retrieve a dog-eared book which exactly encapsulated whatever point he was making. He seemed to know those books off by heart, and I wondered how someone who enjoyed drinking and roistering as much as Nico could find time to become so erudite in so many areas of academic endeavour.

The zips on my tent had long since given up the ghost and I used to drape a mosquito net over the entrance to make sure I wasn't bitten. That night I tucked the net into place before sinking into a deep, contented sleep. In the morning, despite my hangover, I noticed immediately that my net was not in place. Living with an almost obsessive fear of mosquitoes, my first reaction was panic that I may have been bitten. I quickly checked my exposed parts for any telltale signs and relaxed a bit when I couldn't find any. Making a mental note to remember to replace the net next time I got up for a pee in the night, I reached for my rucksack which always stayed securely at the top end of the tent. Everything I owned of value was in my rucksack and I started to worry when I could not find it. I knocked on Nico's door to ask him if I had left it in his room, with my bike. Even full of sleep, he could tell from my voice that I was anxious and we searched the nooks and crannies of his room, but no joy. Nico kept inviting me to search anywhere I wanted and even lifted up his mattress as proof he had not taken the bag. He was distraught and I was quick to assure him that I didn't think he had stolen from me. Nonetheless, I was getting panicky because everything of importance to me was in the bag—passport, money, travellers' cheques and my diary. My immediate concern was that without a passport I would have to go home and so would not be able to complete my journey.

Esther turned up and Nico asked her if she had seen the bag and although I didn't speak her language, I could tell that she had and was explaining to Nico what had happened. Nico told me that she was saying that Maria had come to the house during the evening, seen the rucksack on the veranda, and had put it in the garage at the bottom of the yard for safety. I was so delighted I could have kissed Esther, but Nico seemed totally unmoved. 'She's just saying that because it's what you want to hear.' It did seem very strange that I had left my precious rucksack out on the veranda but I just wanted to get into the garage to check it out. Unfortunately, it was Maria's garage and only she had a key: we had to find Maria as soon as possible. By now I was beside myself with anxiety and cursing myself for having been so careless, but as I went into my tent I remembered that the net had been moved. As I then found that my trousers and my toilet bag were also missing, I slowly realised that someone must have come into my tent as I slept. With a sinking feeling, I came to the conclusion that to search the garage was just clutching at straws, but I was still desperate to do it, so we set off to find Maria.

Nico reckoned that the best place to start looking would be the taxi rank just outside the Central Market where Boris and Maria had a small office. On the way we called in to a bakery to get some bread for breakfast, because even at a time like this, my appetite was undiminished. In the bakery was a middle-aged, hippyish European woman, the only white person I had seen in Inhambane apart from Nico. She spoke enthusiastically about a huge rave that was due to be held on the beach the following day, with over a thousand people expected. Nico, predictably, was very interested but I was preoccupied and when asked if I would be going said probably not. The woman was amazed that I could be in Inhambane and not go to such a momentous event. A week later, in Maputo, I met the DJ from the event and in fact over two thousand people turned up. He was at the British High Commission getting a new passport because he too was robbed, the morning after the rave. He had lost hundreds of CDs from his car and was inconsolable.

At the taxi rank we found Boris in a very smart mini-bus and Nico asked him where he could find Maria. The hostility and contempt between the two men was almost visible and I realised that it was asking quite a lot of Nico to seek assistance of any kind from the one person he really hated. Maria was out on a job but Boris had a garage key and was prepared to lend it to us, provided it was "brought straight back, and no messing." From the off, I shared Nico's dislike of Boris; he was a big, ugly man, patronising and unfriendly. Some people might say he was typically German but he wasn't—he was too boorish and too aggressive. He was so much the opposite of Nico that I wondered how one woman could have fallen for both men, and I was left with the impression that Maria must have a high regard for money.

In my head I knew Nico was right about Esther's story but nevertheless I was still bitterly disappointed when our search of the garage proved fruitless. I found it hard to get my head around why Esther should make up such a silly and time wasting tale, but Nico said it was not at all unusual. It was just her way of trying to make me feel better and of course for a little while, she did.

After my run in with the army in Zimbabwe, I felt uncomfortably vulnerable without a passport, but my most urgent requirement was to get some money. Nico took me to a Western Union bank in town where they have a link to American Express, who issued my travellers' cheques. Eventually, I got to see the manager who told me, through Nico, that she had never heard of any link to American Express and that there was no way she could help me. It took me over a week to get replacement cheques and I was completely underwhelmed by the slow and suspicious response I was to get when eventually I was able to make contact with American Express. Despite my predicament, they were unhelpful, inefficient and very unfriendly.

At the Police Station, the only place where Nico did not appear to be well known, we were made to wait for the rest of the morning until I could make a statement. This would have been impossible without Nico, as not one officer spoke a word of English, but well worth it because I now had a piece of paper to explain the absence of a passport. Even so I had to spend my last few coins getting it photocopied, as the police would not let me keep the original.

While we waited, Nico asked me what I planned to do, and I explained that I would have to go to Maputo, the capital, to replace my passport and travellers' cheques. He asked what I was going to do for money and I thought I could sell either my tent or my bike. Reluctantly, I decided it would have to be the bike, as to get to Maputo quickly I would need to take the bus, and in any case my bike was broken. Nico asked how much I wanted for the bike and I said about two million metacais—about eighty US dollars. He said maybe he could get Maria to buy it for him, he would say that it would provide the transport for a fictitious job he was going to get. He gave away a lot about their relationship by saying that, but I was happy to go along with it.

As it was lunchtime, Maria would be at home and we walked to the smart new home that she had once shared with Nico. She lived in the best part of town, the houses had walled gardens and burglar alarms and the roads were tarred. Maria was on the veranda of her house being served lunch by a servant. She was a large, well-dressed woman in her forties and once would have been very beautiful. She obviously enjoyed her food and did not interrupt her meal, or offer us anything, at any point during our visit.

Nico got to work straight away with his request, adopting a position which was virtually on his knees in front of her. To my surprise, they conducted the conversation in German, and although I don't speak the language, I saw that Maria was vehemently turning him down. However, Nico sneaked me a wink and I knew it was only going to be a matter of time. Eventually, Nico got up and explained that she had relented but only to the tune of one million metacais. Had I known that it would take so long to get money from American Express, I would probably have held out for more but I agreed to the lower price. Maria counted out the money from her purse and we walked back to Nico's place.

On the way we called in at a shebeen where the men were drinking a cloudy substance which tasted a bit like cider and vomit but was quite enjoyable. The women were eating porridge from a huge cooking pot and I asked if I could try some. They gave me a spoon and I left the men to sit with the women and enjoy one of the best meals I had in Africa. As a child I could remember eating a fantastic porridge called mealie meal, made from ground maize, and I had been on the lookout for it during my journey. Today was the first time I had found it and it was every bit as good as I remembered. By the time I finished eating, the amount I had consumed was a source of amazement for everybody in the shebeen, including Nico who had already seen me in action. Fortunately the pot was still half full so I didn't feel too bad, but when I pulled out Maria's money to pay, they wouldn't let me.

Back at the house, I removed the saddlebags and sadly handed my bike over to Nico. He had never ridden a bike with gears so I explained how they worked, and I also showed him the parts that needed to be replaced. I told him a bike was the best way to get around in Africa and he said he was going to keep it so that he could get fit. Apparently, Maria had scoffed at the notion that he would use the bike himself— he would sell it to raise money for beer, and really we both knew she was right. I gave him the lock and key in the hope that with these he would get a better price.

The bus for Maputo left in the morning and there was no reason to change my plans about going to Peace's house to enjoy the banquet. To make matters even easier, the bus stopped just down the road from the beach where he lived. With less than a million metacais in my pocket, however, there was no way I could have stayed on for the rave on the beach.

Nico and I took a minibus taxi, the cheapest form of mechanised transport, to Peace's house. As we waited for the taxi to fill up, I put a five-litre flagon of wine, which I had bought for the party, under the seats with my luggage, as there was no room for it anywhere else. A young man in smart business clothes got in and acknowledged Nico, who warily nodded back. As we set off the young man made a remark which sparked a sudden and furious tirade from Nico. I didn't have a clue what was being said, but did catch the phrase Black and White several times. Soon they were both shouting furiously and from time to time, some of the other passengers would throw in an opinion.

As she rose to get off, a young woman paused to launch an angry verbal attack on the businessman and the other passengers seemed to nod in agreement with her. She got off and after we had got going again, the young man said something placatory to Nico and offered his hand. Nico refused it indignantly but unfortunately burst into tears, and this time everyone was embarrassed. He had told me that the whole town felt he had been badly treated by Boris and Maria, and now I believed him.

As we got off, the passengers had sympathetic words for Nico and patted his arm. They were very helpful to me as I gathered up my luggage. We were halfway across the road when I suddenly remembered the wine I had left under a seat and Nico's sorrows disappeared as he chased the taxi down the road, shouting his head off.

Peace's house was off a sandy track leading to the beach, sheltered by picturesque palm trees and completely surrounded by a waist-high wicket fence. It was constructed entirely of wood and the roof was thatched with palm leaves. There was no electricity and no running water but it was substantial, spotlessly clean and it was furnished with polished hardwood cabinets and comfortable leather sofas. The toilets were outside at the far end of the yard, two covered holes in the ground, and Peace explained which one was for which bodily function.

Peace's wife was a tiny lady who was overjoyed that we were there, and Peace himself told me that it was a great honour for him to have us stay with them. I assured him the honour was all mine. As I was shown where I would be sleeping, a mat on the floor in the living area, I had a moment's anxiety about the lack of mosquito protection but decided that, sod it, for once I would just take a chance. As it happened, by the time I went to bed, I would have slept happily in a snake pit. Nights with Nico the Greek are not abstemious.

Nico had been waiting by the road for the taxi to make its return journey so that he could retrieve the wine, and he came in bearing his prize, his altercation on the way a distant memory. The banquet was a great success, and I was relieved that the pig had been slaughtered long before we arrived. Africa is no place for someone who likes animals, and I had seen some distressing sights but I had not become sufficiently desensitised to relish the prospect of seeing a pig having its throat cut for my dinner. My recollections of the evening are a little hazy, but we were joined by Peace's children and other friends and relatives who were all introduced to me as if I was a visiting dignitary. It didn't seem to matter that I was slurring my words. We toasted Peace's house-building skills and his wife's culinary skills. I asked Nico the word for "friendship" and proposed a toast to that and everyone applauded wildly. The children sang songs that I thought were truly beautiful. When Nico sang an old Greek sea shanty, in his rasping voice, he brought the house down. Eventually the wine ran out and the men moved to a shebeen on the beach and I sat on a palm tree log drinking a spirit that burned my throat like fire. I don't remember going to bed.

Peace woke me in the morning and his wife gave me a hug and a box of fruit for the bus. She also gave me a hand-carved wooden eggcup and I gave her my pliers. Peace, Nico and I walked to where a small group of people were waiting for the bus. As it pulled into view, I felt that I was leaving an old friend in Nico although I had known him only a couple of days. Naturally he was in tears and for some reason he gave me an old recipe book, in which he had written a farewell note in a curiously neat and careful hand. I settled into the only available seat in the packed bus with my luggage on my lap and, waving goodbye to the two guys, I realised with a pang that I had forgotten to give them my compass for their boat.

Chapter 13

The thief who had taken my documentation and money had also taken some more mundane items such as my reading glasses (which I would replace as soon as my travellers' cheques came through) and my trousers. These were special trousers, as they had a zip around the knee so that they could convert from longs into shorts. Feeling conspicuous and vulnerable in my cycling shorts, (in Africa only kids wear shorts) I used some of my precious bike money to replace the trousers. Nico took me to some clothing shops, all run by Asians, where I found some horrible yellow and brown trousers with a zip around the knee. They also had zipped pockets on the thigh which was a major selling point for me, being almost pickpocket-proof. Conscious that I was short of money, I bargained as hard as I could and managed to get a discount of about one percent.

The material of these grotesque trousers was like very thick bin liner and soon the sweat was trickling down my legs on the bus. Halfway to Maputo the bus stopped so that the passengers could use the stinking toilets at a teeming bus station in Xai Xai. We had to walk past women squatting in doorless toilets to get to the urinals. Having long since eaten my gift of fruit, I joined a queue of people waiting to buy bread at a stall. Just as I got to the head I was barged out of the way by a very fat guy from my bus who needed serving quickly because the bus was about to leave. The conductor yelled at me to get on and even seemed to take a kick at me as I was jostled back to my seat. As I sat down, I felt fresh air on my leg and saw that the zips on my trousers had failed. They never worked again and eventually I swapped them for a towel in a market in Maputo, the first time I had possessed a towel in the entire journey.

The journey took about four hours and as we pulled into Maputo, and the bus began to empty, touts banged on the windows and even boarded the bus to insist that they take me to the best, cheapest backpackers in town. They had an aggressive selling style and, feeling very much alone, I turned them all down.

A few weeks before, a lot further north, I had met two white South Africans at a lonely garage where they were filling up with diesel and I was getting water. They were interested in my story and told me that they were civil engineers, on their way to oversee the repair of flood damaged roads in the north. I told them I was planning to go to South Africa, via Maputo, and they gave me the familiar warnings about the crime and violence I could expect to encounter en route. More to the point, they worked from a yard in central Maputo where I would be very welcome to pitch my tent. There were showers and toilets and the whole area was fenced and guarded. They gave me the address and directions, which I wrote into my diary, the same diary that was stolen in Inhambane. All I could remember was that the yard had white gates, was near the railway station and that I was to ask for the foreman, Zak.

Not wishing to carry my bulky cycle panniers around looking for a yard with white gates in a city famous for its street crime, I decided to ask the driver if he could suggest somewhere to stay. He dropped me off at a corner and directed me to a hotel just up the road. As I got there, I could see that there was no way I could afford such luxury; there were flags at the front and the rooms even had TVs in them. Still, I went in and asked the receptionist for the price just to check. Tired and feeling a bit edgy, I would have given anything to stay there but just one night would have taken more than half my money. The receptionist, who was friendly and sympathetic, offered a cheaper rate but I still couldn't afford it and she gave me directions for a nearby backpackers. This was on Avenido Mao Tse Tung (all the major roads were named after revolutionary heroes) and was called Fatima's Place. Oddly enough, Nico had also highly recommended Fatima's Place but I had disregarded it because I assumed it must have been a brothel.

It was an excellent backpackers, good value for money and full of hardcore travellers who seemed to give me a bit of respect now that I had been arrested, robbed and was penniless. I worked out that if I ate nothing but bread and bananas, I could stay at least a week.

The day after I was robbed I phoned Joy to tell her that I had lost my passport and travellers cheques and soon after settling in at Fatima's I phoned her again. To my delight, she had been in touch with the British High Commission and they were expecting me right now, even though it was a Sunday with a national holiday on the Monday. Delighted to have stolen a march on two whole days, I walked the length of Avenido Lenin to the Commission where I was seen by the Vice Counsul who told me I could have a new passport in two days. I could still go to South Africa and I could still complete my journey. The next task was to get my cheques replaced and this was to prove much harder. Without the two hours access to a telephone kindly donated by the Vice Consul, it would literally have been impossible, as I did not have the money to pay for international phone calls. It was my first experience of American Express and the thought occurred to me that travellers are usually in trouble when they need to have their cheques replaced. I was staggered that they made it so difficult.

My next task was to take my passport to the Immigration Office to get a new visa and I was looking for it in a rather run down part of the city when I saw two policemen and I asked for directions. One of them was about to point out the way to go when the other demanded to see my passport. He had twigged from my destination that I must have some form of irregularity in my documentation and my heart sank as I handed over my visa-less passport. He quizzed me hard for about ten minutes before his partner persuaded him to let me continue. I reminded myself that when you are in trouble, never involve the police.

The clerk at the office was typical of the type of official who will always give you a hard time. Fat, aggressive and stupid, he made me wait for two hours because his chief was not there. He was the type you dread if you need a bit of sympathetic co-operation. All he wanted was to show me how he called the shots and that I was in his power. Eventually he took my passport and told me to come back at 10 a.m. the next day. I was there at 9 a.m. and waited until midday to be told that his chief had been too busy and told me to come back at 10 a.m. the next day. At 10 a.m. the next day, he said his boss was in a meeting and I spent another couple of hours in the bare, dreary waiting room. Every hour or so I would ask the clerk how much longer I would have to wait, which was just what he wanted, but I couldn't help myself.

At lunchtime I went out to get something to eat and when I came back, I saw a man in a suit go upstairs past the waiting room and through a large wooden door. I guessed he was the boss and followed him, my indignation and sense of grievance lending me a bit of courage. The room contained five men around a table with one man at a desk at the top. Like me, they seemed surprised by my audacity in marching in. Addressing the man at the desk, the man I had seen climb the stairs, I asked if my visa was ready, as I had been waiting three days. He said something to one of the guys at the table who actually seemed embarrassed. He produced a file and handed the boss my passport and two pieces of paper which the boss signed and stamped and gave to me with a smile and an apology for the inconvenience. I wasn't even asked to pay, and as I walked downstairs I could not resist waving my prize in the face of my fat friend and thanking him for his assistance. To make the moment even sweeter, he looked shocked rigid that my documents had been processed and that I had what I wanted. I gave him the award for the most heartfelt scowl in Africa.

Out in the street I saw the two policemen and the friendly one called me over and gave me the local handshake that involves grabbing the thumb and clicking the middle finger as it is released. It's quite complicated but feels very friendly. The nasty one never even acknowledged me.

Walking back towards the city centre, I came upon the railway station and I had a look for the white gates of the civil engineering yard. Finding them without difficulty, I asked the guards if I could see Zak and they took me in. The compound was clean, well maintained and there was a beautiful patch of flat, green grass, perfect for my tent. Zak was a burly Afrikaner in his early thirties who had already been phoned by the guys I had met up north to tell him I would be coming. He dismissed out of hand any notion that I should camp in the grounds, saying he would take me home with him and I could stay there as long as I liked. He had a girlfriend who would be glad of the company.

My preference would have been to stay in the city, as I still had my travellers' cheques to sort out and I was using the High Commission's telephone and their address, but Zak was adamant. We agreed that I would go back to Fatima's Place, get my things and come back at five when he left for home. We drove home in his bakkie and I was introduced to Elvey. Plump, blonde and quite pretty, she was a lot younger than Zak and I got the impression that her constant inane chatter got under his skin sometimes. My presence would take some of the pressure off him. Elvey sat me down and got out two huge scrapbooks which she had compiled over the years. Zak quietly slipped out. They were full of arty farty drawings and obscure poems which she had written at art school. There were also photos of her in studied poses that she invited me to admire. The whole thing was tedious beyond belief, but she was animated and just as Zak had suggested, she was very glad of the company. At one point she asked me if I knew how Rhodesia had got its name. I told her yes, I did know, from Cecil Rhodes. She then proceeded to explain where the name came from and even asked me if I understood. They were a hospitable and generous couple and I was keen to get to know some Afrikaans people, as I had never got acquainted with Afrikaners before. It was also very nice to have somewhere to stay until the cheques came through, as I was just about broke by now. But as Elvey babbled on I did rather regret that American Express were proving so difficult and so longwinded.

Zak's company provided the house and the car and also paid for two house boys, who worked twelve-hour shifts around the clock so that there was always someone there for security. Zak and Elvey's relationship with "the boys" was a reminder of the South Africa I had left as a child in the sixties. They never asked them to do anything, instructions were always given as orders—I never heard a "please" or a "thank you." Whenever Zak arrived in his car one of the boys would run to open the gate. I always wondered why they had to run to do this job, and I felt it summed up the demeaning nature of the relationship. Just like the South Africans of my youth, they were disparaging about the abilities of the blacks and accepted their own innate superiority effortlessly. They were never cruel to their boys but woe betide the one who fell asleep during the night when he was supposed to be guarding the house, or who didn't hear the horn sound when Zak wanted the gate opened.

Zak had a big trial's bike which was his pride and joy. Occasionally he would leave it on the drive rather than put it away in the garage, particularly if he had been tinkering with it, which he did a lot probably in an effort to gain some respite from Elvey. It was a spectacular motorcycle of a type not often seen in Mozambique, and it made Zak laugh when his boys begged him to lock it out of sight in the garage. As the guards, they were afraid that they would be killed by any thief who took a fancy to it, and I could see their point. Zak dismissed their fears but he knew that violent crime was an everyday occurrence and he rarely put himself or Elvey at risk. The local bottle store was only half a mile away but he would always take his car for security reasons. In fact neither of them ever walked anywhere in Mozambique. Naturally, they thought I was completely out of my mind.

One Sunday, Elvey and Zak wanted to take me for a drive to a beautiful beach about twenty miles up the coast. As we drove along the coastal track to the beach we saw groups of children who would dance for the few coins the tourists chucked at them. Elvey had a game that she never tired of. We would stop the car, call over the kids as if to ask them to dance and suddenly she would produce a rubber snake which caused panic in the kids. Then we drove off, laughing heartily but without having given any money. I felt really bad about being involved in this insulting charade and when Elvey asked me if I wanted to have a go, I said no. Even Zak seemed to feel it was getting a bit tiresome but he said nothing. On the beach, Elvey pranced up to groups of blacks to frighten them and the game continued as we drove home, with any blacks on the road. Driving through a township, she stuck the snake into the face of a youth who had the presence of mind not to shriek and run off but to grab it. With this show of pride and quick thinking, the youth not only brought the game to a welcome end but also salvaged much of the dignity of his own people.

Eventually, my cheques came through and I wanted to take my hosts out to a bar in town that they liked, to celebrate my last night. Elvey was disappointed that I was not staying longer, but in truth some of her childish ways were getting on my nerves. Instead of using a phrase like "and so on and so forth" she would babble "and worra worra worra" and she did this so regularly that eventually I couldn't stand it. It was definitely time to move on. I cashed my first travellers cheque since the robbery and put the money in the zipped pocket of the trousers I had bought in Inhambane, the ones which I thought were pickpocket-proof. At the bar we met some of their friends and I offered to get in the first round. As I went to undo the zip on my pocket I realised that it was open and with a sinking feeling I felt for the money. I had not spent a penny of it and already it had been stolen. It was only fifty dollars but I felt almost as bad as when I was robbed the first time, particularly as Zak then had to pay for the drinks.

The next day I cashed more cheques and bought a single-speed African bike with a huge rack to which I attached my luggage and set off for the border with South Africa. My feelings towards Zak and Elvey were mixed. Gratitude for their friendly and spontaneous hospitality, which was given freely at a time when I did need it. True, Elvey had irritated me a lot but as I was taking my leave, I softened towards her and put a lot of her silliness down to loneliness. She didn't work and while Zak was away she passed most days alone in their house. Mainly, I felt disappointed by their ingrained, immovable racism, even though I was beginning to understand it better.

Chapter 14

When I had first triumphantly picked up my renewed visa I had not realised that the border crossing point was specified, and that the specified crossing point was a long way from the point I had originally intended entering South Africa. I knew I would get no help from the fat clerk if I tried to get it altered, so from Maputo I cycled east to Komantipoort, rather than south to Ressano Garcia. It was a good road with a wide hard shoulder where I felt reasonably safe. However, crossing the border was a nightmare, largely because when I had been given two pieces of paper at the Immigration Office in Maputo, I had naively thought that one was for the authorities and the other was a spare. In fact the irritable border clerk wanted them both and unfortunately I had mislaid the copy. For some reason, my apparent stupidity drove him into a tantrum and I struggled to keep up with the gist of what he was shouting at me. As was usually the case with any government office, the place was packed with people all trying their best to get what they needed, and I found it difficult to work out what the hell was going on. It was just like this every time I went to a government office in Africa—it always reminded me of last orders at the pub, without the beer but with plenty of people ready for a fight.

Eventually the matter was settled in the time-honoured way, with a bribe. I had to pay for a photocopy, which cost about twenty pounds and so was allowed to exit.

At the South African side, I was held up at the window because the black female clerk seemed to be confused by the fact that my passport had been issued in Maputo and my birthplace was South Africa. I tried to explain that I was "just a tourist from England" but she was having none of it. Eventually she called over a guard who marched me back to the Mozambican side where the sight of me aroused my aggressive friend to even greater heights of anger. He told me I would have to go back to Maputo to get my documents sorted out properly, and turned his back. For the first time, my anger started to bubble up and I shouted back that there was no way I was going back to fucking Maputo, and I walked the fifty yards back to the queue of people trying to get into South Africa. When I got to the woman, I blurted out that just because she had not bothered to understand what I was trying to say to her, I had to go back to Maputo. This was a kind of plea to her better nature and I suppose sometimes it might have worked, but not today. She laughed, literally, in my face and turned away.

In all my time in Africa, I had not had to retrace my steps to any significant degree; like any cyclist I dreaded the very idea of having to go back. On this occasion, my aversion was even greater—I would have to go back to the fat bastard at the Immigration Office and throw myself on his mercy. No doubt my face expressed the utter horror of my situation and to my surprise another clerk came over and motioned me to give him my passport. He had a rather pleasant face and he studied it for a while and then produced a miracle. He told me to make my way through a large crowd of people who were waiting for customs control and come into the office. This was a queue easily an hour long, if not longer, and as I barged through, a white guy called out, "What the fuck do you think you are doing?" I turned round and shouted, "Look, mate, I don't know what the fuck is going on!" He just shrugged his shoulders, maybe feeling that I had had enough hassle for one day.

Inside the office the pleasant guy was waiting with another officer with my passport. He asked me a few easy questions like where was I going, where had I been born and what was my mother's name. With a smile he said there was no problem and waved me through.

Reflecting on all this, and all the other times African officialdom had made life difficult for me, I realised firstly that at no point had anyone really made life impossible. After all, I had not actually been sent back to Maputo. It had been a minor altercation at the border which would not even have ranked on the Richter scale of some travellers. Whenever I had been forced into needing something I had always got it eventually, be it a visa or a visa replacement or permission to cross a roadblock. There are "jobsworths" all over the world, who, as soon as they know you need something from them, will wallow in their power over you. Everyone knows it is not personal and to get offended or frustrated is just silly. It's just that in Africa, you immediately fall back on the old postcolonial conception that "they are getting their own back." So you are reminded that not long ago your ancestors exploited and brutalised their ancestors, and, if you are alone and feeling just a bit vulnerable, this is just one more thing to make you feel a little less comfortable.

There are lots of things in Africa that have this effect. You get it when white people warn you about blacks or when you see or hear of crime, or AIDS or poverty. But I remember thinking, as I rode into South Africa, how the black woman laughed in my face and how disappointed I was to feel so unwelcome as I entered my destination country. Without a doubt, the country that disappointed me most in Africa was South Africa, and that was probably because it was the country from which I had expected the most.

From my armchair in the UK I had watched as Nelson Mandela was elected President in free and fair elections and how the Springboks had won the 1995 Rugby World Cup. Mandela and Francois Pienaar had shown the trophy to the Rainbow Nation and Francois had said it was not won for the sixty-five thousand in the stadium but for the forty-eight million people in South Africa. It was a time of huge optimism and for the first time I had felt pride in the country of my birth. Having conquered the rugby world it was only a matter of time before we conquered the football world. As I made my way through Africa, through the corruption and chaos towards South

Africa, I consoled myself with the thought that when I got there things would be different. There would be a first-world infrastructure, decent roads, police, supermarkets, cafes, clean campsites. Most of all I was looking forward to a place where I would not have to keep on my toes all the time and where I did not feel constantly that it was me against them.

The disappointment came even before I set foot in South Africa. I saw a white South African family on a camping holiday in Mozambique being waited on hand and foot by the black couple who were their servants. The black guy not only erected the tents but also cooked the barbecue. I struggled to see the logic in having servants put up your tent on a camping holiday, but to hand over the pleasures of the braai—now that was as illogical as it was dismaying. This sense that the Rainbow Nation was not necessarily what I had imagined was confirmed when I saw how Zak and Elvey related to their "boys" in Maputo and even more so when I got my warnings from white people I met on the road. They would tell me that the blacks I may have encountered on my travels through Africa were not like "our blacks." The blacks in South Africa were considered to be just as inferior as the blacks in the rest of Africa but different because of the intensity of their hatred for the whites. Sometimes when I heard whites talking about "our blacks" in this way, I got the impression that they were almost proud of the ruthless streak they were referring to which other African blacks did not have. Proud in the way that some English football fans are proud that their club's hooligans are more notorious than those of another club.

I couldn't blame the blacks for their hatred and I could sympathise with the fear that the white has of the black, but it was clear that between them little progress had been made towards the ideals of the Rainbow Nation. So when the first black African I met in South Africa laughed in my face at my discomfiture, I was bitterly disappointed.

As I have pointed out earlier, it is the people you meet on a journey who colour your views of the experience much more than the terrain you see or the food you eat. Each time I met someone who was friendly, or who rendered a service without demanding a reward, I felt good and my confidence and morale would lift. Where people were unfriendly, obstructive or grasping, the opposite effect kicked in but to a far greater extent. Whilst in Africa I had many more positive encounters than negative ones, but the effects of the latter were far more pervasive and far more profound. In South Africa and Swaziland, I had too many of these to counteract the effects of all the friendliness and hospitality I was shown.

My lowest moments usually occurred during the hour or so before dusk when I would start to look for somewhere safe to sleep, particularly if I was a long way from a town or a campsite. At these times I often got homesick. In the morning, after a night's sleep and with a whole day ahead, I would feel much less vulnerable and generally quite optimistic.

Towards the end of a day in Swaziland, I stopped at a fork in the road to look at my map to see which was the best route to take. My vulnerability level was neutral, as for the previous few days I had had neither positive nor negative encounters with anyone. Unfortunately, the new bicycle was not running well because the mountain range I had crossed to enter Swaziland from South Africa had been very hard on the rear hub, which also housed the brake. Coming down the steep untarred roads had caused severe overheating and now strange noises were coming from that area. Whenever my bike was below par I felt the same.

As I studied the map for the road which would take me back into South Africa, I noticed a group of youths sitting on the roadside fence. One of them slid off and crossed the road towards me. Feeling a little uneasy, I smiled and asked him if he knew which was the best road to take for the border. He ignored the question and said something that sent a chill through me. He said, "The boys are not happy that you're here."

Wishing that I had not stopped, and weighing up whether I could pedal off without being caught, I asked him why they were unhappy that I was there. He was about to reply when we were joined by another, younger youth, perhaps fourteen or fifteen years old, who started berating me for being a racist. He was a decent-looking sort of lad, wearing a tie, and very articulate but the more he carried on the more excited he became. He was asking me why the whites hated the blacks and why we were more racist now than ever before. Looking at the first guy, who was the bigger of the two, I said that I was not a racist, I was just trying to get to the border but if he couldn't help I would just go. I wasn't sure if my bike could get me away as quickly as I wanted. To my relief, he pointed along one road saying that both led to the border but that this one was new and so would be an easier ride. With my hub grinding away, I set off as directed.

The information I had been given was correct and the road was good but it was nearly dusk and I had been unnerved by the episode. I decided that I would not pitch my tent that night unless I found somewhere that was completely safe. It is times like this that you wish that you had a companion.

As I rounded a hillside, I noticed a little homestead on a hilltop. There were two youngsters coming down a path to the road. I stopped and asked them if I could put my tent amongst their huts. They seemed incredulous at my request and their excitement attracted the attention of a couple of guys in long brown overcoats, who were waiting at a bus stop down the road. The overcoats came over to ask me what I wanted, and I explained. They said they would show me a place where I could sleep but I really didn't like the look of them and turned back to the lads and repeated my request. They were obviously from the homestead and looked decent. The older of the two was called Pius and he took me up the path and into the homestead, where I immediately became the centre of attention.

Pius proudly introduced me to the family elders and, feeling that I had made the right decision, I began to relax. Pius' mother insisted that I park my bike inside her hut for safety. Pius told me where I could erect my tent and as I did so, I was surrounded by a dozen curious kids who watched my every move. I could not even have a pee without them staring openly at me. Being the centre of attention is a small price to pay for a vast improvement in security, and I bantered with them for an hour or so, basically trying to learn and pronounce their names, which caused great hilarity. Disconcertingly, the two guys from the bus stop had moved to a rock at the bottom of the hill and were also watching closely. However, with all the attention I was getting, I felt fairly safe. Then I told them I was really tired, which I was, and crawled into my tent. As I lay in my bag, groups of people were shown my tent and for a long time I could hear them walking around it and discussing me. From time to time I could hear the sounds of revelry and it was clear that some of the homestead were getting pretty plastered. On every occasion that I camped inside a village, I seemed to hit party night. I never experienced a time when everyone just went quietly to bed, but am not sure if they had a bender because I had arrived or because they had a bender every night. Looking back on it, maybe I should have gone and joined them sometimes but being alone and uninvited, I never did.

I didn't see the two guys in overcoats again, but I wonder if their offer of a place to stay was genuine or a prelude to mischief. There were so many times when I treated strangers as potential enemies and never got to find out if I was right or wrong. I suspect on this occasion, though, I was probably right.

Very early in the morning, much before I normally woke up, the two lads from the homestead were banging on the side of my tent and Pius was unzipping the door. He told me he was coming in and I told him he was not. They were excited rather than aggressive but I would have preferred the opportunity to wake in my own good time. Clambering out, I greeted them warmly and we all shook hands. Other kids started appearing and I took another self-conscious pee and packed up my tent, a bit piqued by my enforced early rising. Pius took me to my bike and as I was attaching my luggage he produced another bike which he invited me to admire. It was an old green mountain bike with very cheap components, but to his delight, I told him it was better than mine. To be honest, it probably was—at least he had some gears. In the manner of someone telling me I had won the lottery, he announced that he was going to ride with me, and I thanked him profusely, beginning to wish that I had camped in the bush after all.

I wanted to thank his mother and the elders for agreeing to let me stay but Pius said it was better not to wake them, confirming my impression that there had been a pretty heavy session the previous night. Before we set off down the path to the road, I gave Pius my last baseball cap and my sunglasses, confident that I could replace them in affluent South Africa. I had broken the sunglasses in Mali whilst I was with the three French guys. Francois had fixed them with plastic cement just before he had gone down with malaria.

Pius and I rode for about an hour on a well-made, almost deserted, road. He told me that his father had died of AIDS and that he was at school but would soon be expelled, as his mother could not afford the fees. Just as we were passing a roadside advert offering "cheap coffins," he told me he would be able to finish his "journey of education" if I gave him ten pounds. I had to admire his timing and I did not disbelieve his story but I told him I could not help him, as I needed my money to complete my own journey. A cap and my only pair of sunglasses would have to be sufficient payment for a night of security, if not peace—and he had knocked me up at the crack of dawn. We parted amicably although I think he had hoped for a better dividend.

My road took me through beautiful deserted countryside, with swooping descents down to bridges over ravines and long slow climbs back up again. Some twenty miles from Mbabane, the capital, the bike started making loud screeching noises and I started feeling uncomfortable that the few people on the road were beginning to stare. During a particularly long and noisy descent to a bridge, the hub started to grind and stick and reluctantly I had to dismount. There was a group of youths by the bridge at a stall selling wooden statues and naturally they soon gathered round me. They were a rough-looking bunch and there was a strong smell of ganja in the air. One of them grabbed the bike and said he was a mechanic and would fix it. Another put his face in mine and said, "He is good mechanic." I said not to bother, as I was going to push it to Mbabane, but in truth the hub was so tight it was hard to push. In any case they were so insistent that it was futile to resist and I took off my two bags so they could stand it upside down. With the bags in my possession, I was thinking that if they decided to make off with the bike I could probably hitch a lift to the city, buy another bike and start again.

With as much serenity as I could muster I thought "sod it" and plonked myself down on the wall of the bridge, wishing someone would offer me a drag of his joint. Soon the ubiquitous hammer and chisel appeared and amidst the usual banging and arguing, the wheel was removed and the hub was disembowelled. The "mechanic" then crossed the road and disappeared for a few minutes to reappear with an old tin of grease. I began to assume a bit of interest, as just maybe it was actually getting mended, but lost it as they started arguing about how to put it all back together again. Then the mechanic stood up, righted the bike and with a triumphant air pushed it towards me. It didn't squeak at all. Beaming, he mounted the bike and rode off across the bridge. From the far side he put up an arm as if waving goodbye and disappeared from view. The others burst out laughing and for some reason I also found it funny and laughed with them. Twenty minutes later he had not reappeared and I noticed that I had not seen a single vehicle. It was going to take a long time to hitch to Mbabane.

As I was about to lug my gear to the roadside to get ready to hitch, he reappeared on the bridge, rode up and handed me the bike. My delight was unbounded; I had not been harmed and I had not been robbed. Even more than that I had the joy that every cyclist experiences when his bike which was broken is now fixed. I gave him an unopened, expensive box of teabags, shook his hand warmly and thanked him from the bottom of my heart. Maybe he had changed his mind about stealing the bike or maybe he was just playing games with me, but we were good mates now, and he was King of the Hill. Not only had he fixed my bike, but he had put me in my place in the best possible way. As I rode off, he was showing off his teabags to his adoring friends.

The bike didn't make it quite as far as Mbabane but at least I was within an hour's walk before it finally gave up the ghost. I checked into the Flying Rhino backpackers where I camped on the lawn and took my bike in to the local modern cycle shop. The mechanic showed me the burnt-out hub and replaced it with a new one. This was the first time in Africa that I had seen a job being done on my bike with tools other than a hammer and chisel. The beautiful blonde lady who ran the shop asked me why on earth I had chosen such a basic bike (she referred to it as a "Hunter") when I could have bought a modern bike with gears. I explained that when I had bought it, it was the only bike with a luggage rack. Even in her shop, fully stocked with the latest gear, there was not a luggage rack for sale. In this part of the world, it is only Africans who carry luggage on bikes—white cyclists only cycle "on tour" and have an organised tour bus to carry their gear. Nobody goes off on their own with a tent and a bike (nobody sane that is), so nobody needs a luggage rack.

Back at the backpackers, I passed the afternoon with a young East German girl called Sara Marie who was wearing native headgear, which rather suited her. A hardcore lone traveller but without the usual pretensions, she told me she had worked as a waitress in Cape Town and was using her earnings to tour Swaziland and South Africa. She had been particularly keen to see the "Reed Dance," a festival where the King of Swaziland chooses maidens for his harem, which had taken place a couple of days previously. She was now heading for Pretoria where a friend had lined up more waitressing work for her. A middle-aged guy who seemed to be a travelling salesman and regularly stayed at the hostel said he was going back to Jo'burg in the morning and he would be happy to drop her off in Pretoria. She accepted the offer gladly and no doubt he was happy to have the company of a pretty young girl on his return trip. That evening a group of young South African lads turned up in a transit van with "Hang Glide Africa" emblazoned on the side. They were on their way to Tanzania to set up a hang-gliding business and within an hour Sara Marie had abandoned her Pretoria plans and had taken up the offer of a spare place in the transit. She had never been to Tanzania before and was delighted by the prospect. Her carefree, unpretentious approach reminded me of Grant, the Kiwi I had last seen in Mauritania. She was a genuine free spirit but without the need to make that claim for herself. Happy to take anything from anyone, she would never become dependent in the way that Grant's Leslie had. I wished her all the best, but her travelling salesman was very disappointed.

Once over the border at Piet Retief and back into South Africa, I rode past the Boer War battlefields towards Ladysmith, the town of my birth. I had left at the age of two months and never been back until now. A couple of miles outside the town, two guys in a bakkie stopped and were horrified when I told them I was cycling to Cape Town and, no, I was not carrying a gun. Despite my protests, they manhandled the bike into the back and drove me to Ladysmith, where I would be safe. On the way they told me the most horrific tales of gratuitous violence inflicted on whites by blacks and insisted that whites simply do not travel the countryside unless in the safety of a vehicle, and in possession of a weapon. No sooner had he said this than we saw an elderly white gentleman in running singlet jogging along the side of the road. He did not appear to be armed. Reading my thoughts, the driver told me he must be a madman, but I must admit I felt much better for seeing him.

Ladysmith was a dump; the municipal campsite was unkempt and run by a black guy who asked if I had "anything I didn't want." The only other residents were a family in a beaten-up caravan who were still there only because their car had broken down. I asked if they would keep an eye on my tent while I had a look around the town but they suggested I either take it with me or stay put.

There was a museum in the centre of the town with an old cannon outside. I asked a young black guy to take my picture and he refused but I bullied him into it. When I had the picture developed, most of it consisted of a huge, black, petulant thumb. If I had expected a civic reception I was disappointed but I thought at least I could visit the museum. Being Sunday it was closed. The following day was a bank holiday and still the museum was closed. I decided to move on.

It would be misleading to suggest that South Africans were either unfriendly or uninterested in me; in fact they were quite the opposite. I had free meals in cafes, free use of the internet and people would often arrange for me to have my picture taken for a story in the local paper. I had more offers of a lift than I can remember. But it was always white or Asian people—I had no social interaction with a black person at any time in South Africa, and I found this very disappointing. I enjoyed the "celebrity status" which I gained for a while in South

Africa but, to my surprise, I missed the cheery waves and greetings which I had got used to in other parts of Africa.

On the road to Pietermaritzburg, the home of my lovely Aunt Geraldine, I was caught up by a group of nineteen cyclists on a five-hundred-mile charity ride. They invited me to have lunch with them and even interviewed me for their tour video. They had a tour manager, two mechanics, a physiotherapist and a load of spare parts in the back up vehicle. The physio confided that the tour manager had stopped for me because I was wearing a bright orange tee shirt. He had interpreted this as a defiant political gesture (apparently orange is an Afrikaans colour) but in fact the shirt was just a freebie given to me by the lady in the modern bike shop. I decided not to wear it anymore. Every night the riders' bikes were washed and checked by the mechanics while they had physio treatment.

I was invited to ride with them and when I struggled to keep up they put me in the most aerodynamic part of the peloton where I was virtually dragged along. That night I camped for free in the grounds of their hotel in a town called Nottingham Road. The next morning they were all off again before daybreak, an amazing feat considering the previous night's alcohol intake. I waved them off and went back to bed for another couple of hours.

A few days later I met another cycle tour of about thirty school children who were cycling from Jo'burg to Durban, where they were to be received by the Lord Mayor. The kids clamoured round me asking all sorts of questions about my trip and my "awesome" single-speed bike. They begged me to ride with them but the tour manager quietly took me aside and asked me to piss off, as I was "raining on their parade." I could see his point and, a bit crestfallen, I sloped off.

In Pietermaritzburg I spent a couple of days with my aunt and when I had eaten her out of house and home, I set off to Durban, where my youngest brother, Steve, lives. The two cities are connected by an annual race called the "Comrades," through fifty-six miles of beautiful scenery and, following the same route, I arrived in downtown Durban in the early evening. My elder brother, Phil, had done the Comrades run some years previously, taking just under eleven hours. After getting lost in some very affluent Durban suburbs (due to my misguided reluctance to use the motorway into town) I covered the distance in a time only marginally better than my brother's. Steve came to pick me up in his four by four and complimented me on my tramp-like appearance, which he maintained was perfectly pitched for avoiding the attentions of muggers.

Steve had to attend his neighbourhood watch meeting that evening and invited me to go along. It was a fascinating insight into the fear of crime that is so deep rooted in white South Africans. Back in the UK, I belonged to a similar scheme but so far have been too apathetic to attend even one meeting. In Steve's locality everyone went: even if your long lost brother has just turned up on a bicycle, you do not miss the neighbourhood watch.

To accommodate the numbers, the local tennis clubroom had been hired; it was packed and every person was white. Each night between the hours of 2 a.m. and 6 a.m., an armed group of four volunteers patrols the streets and gardens of the neighbourhood on a strict rota basis. They report any incidents to the Chairman who reports back to this meeting. I listened to an account of when the guys heard a noise in someone's garden and found a black woman eating something she had scavenged from the bins. She had pleaded her innocence and they had sent her on her way. More sinister and more chilling was the report of how they had come across a black guy who told them he was on his way to the hospital. As his story did not tally with the geography of the area, they concluded he was a burglar on the prowl. To involve the police is considered a pointless waste of time so they exacted their own punishment and the four whites beat up the guy and chucked him out the neighbourhood. Afterwards, Steve and I discussed this and he told me that he had also been involved in vigilante beatings of this nature, and that he felt extremely uncomfortable about it. However, he didn't see a better way of dealing with the problem and I couldn't suggest one either. The strategy may reduce the risk of being robbed in their neighbourhood, but by definition it only increases the risk in another one. More tellingly, it can only reinforce the hatred and fear between the races. During the evening I heard such tales of violence and hatred, often told in totally dispassionate tones, that inwardly I laughed at my naivety and ignorance in once believing so passionately in the ideals of the "Rainbow Nation."

In Durban I was still a thousand miles short of my destination in Cape Town and I was feeling so disillusioned about the reality I had found in South Africa that I was ready to switch my destination to Durban. The last leg just seemed like a pointless and dangerous slog. Phil had lived in Cape Town for twenty years but during my journey to him, he had left South Africa to live in the UK. This gave Steve the opportunity to take the piss out of me and we both had a laugh, but Phil's absence also added to the sense of anti-climax I was feeling. After all, he was the reason why Cape Town was my original destination.

Steve was just a few years younger than me, but a few years earlier, at the age of forty, he had made an extraordinary discovery about himself. He had a real talent for painting, and with the aid of a few lessons, he had become one of the most promising artists in South Africa. I am no expert but Steve's work was obviously very good and his paintings were often on display at the leading galleries. He also had a thriving stall at a local craft market and he sold paintings on the internet. Apart from the fulfilment he got from his art, Steve was no longer confined to a routine nine-to-five life and had gained real independence. To my amazement and delight, he suggested he should borrow a bike and ride with me to Cape Town. In a moment, the last leg had gone from a pointless slog to the final climax of the adventure.

A couple of days later Steve and I were waved off by his friends, his beautiful Indian girlfriend, Cheryl, and his daughter Jenna. They all thought he had gone totally mad so I hesitate to imagine what they thought of me.

Steve always maintained that he had decided to come with me because he wanted to share the adventure. I suspect that he felt that, on my own, I would not have made it. On reflection, I am sure he was right.

Only 25 miles out of Durban we were attacked by four guys who tried to rob us at knifepoint. We managed to prevail, thanks only to the incredible bravery of a lone female motorist who stopped as we grappled in the middle of the road. No doubt assuming she had a gun, our assailants fled empty-handed. Had I been on my own at that point I would have lost my possessions for sure, and given what I now know about the nature of crime in South Africa, maybe my life as well.

Apart from a few bumps and bruises, Steve and I were unhurt but both of us were a bit shaken. From then on we cycled only on the hard shoulder of the motorway, as we felt reassured by the greater number of cars. Cycling through or near townships always made us feel uneasy but we had no further need to physically defend ourselves.

Once we got beyond Port Elizabeth and onto the Garden Route, the atmosphere changed dramatically and for the rest of the journey we felt completely unthreatened. This is a tourist region with no townships to negotiate and the settlements along the coast are all very white and very middle class. For me it was probably the tamest part of my African trip, but I was ready for tame and I thoroughly enjoyed that aspect of it. The Garden Route is so named because of the display of wild flowers growing alongside the road, and this, coupled with the sea and mountain views, makes it probably the most spectacular ride I have ever experienced. Being with my brother and eating and sleeping in predominantly tourist establishments, I felt more "on holiday" than at any previous time. Steve had not been on a bike since he was fifteen so we took it easy and often walked up the bigger hills, although he soon found his cycle legs. In this environment we had many opportunities to sample the great South African wines which we didn't pass up very often. My appetite for food was undiminished—for the first time since leaving home I actually put on some weight.

At a little town called Humansdorp we asked a big, rather fierce-looking Afrikaner where we could find a food store. He seemed a bit preoccupied but asked what kind of food were we looking for. Steve said something to braai and beer and wine—our staple diet. Just as we set off to follow his instructions, he asked if we had a driver's license. Steve said he had and the man called us back and said he had a proposition. He had a car which needed to be towed to a village up in the mountains, but the person who had agreed to steer it had let him down. If Steve would do it, he would put us up for the night at his farm, feed us and buy us beer and wine. To top it off, in the morning, he would also take us and our bikes up to the top of the mountain pass so we could freewheel all the way back down to the Garden Route. We agreed readily, and he asked us what we drank—red wine for me and beer for Steve. He told us to wait while he went to the shop to buy the food and booze. His name was Henke, and soon Steve and I took to referring to him as "Henke the Liar."

With Steve in the tow car, which was attached to Henke's Land Rover with an old piece of rope that broke twice, we eventually made it to an old Boer village, so high in the mountains that it felt appreciably colder. There was not much of interest apart from a quaint white church where, apparently, P W Botha was buried. We dropped the car off at the village garage and drove back to Henke's huge farm, about an hour away. Henke looked just like an overgrown schoolboy and never stopped talking about the size of his farm and how much he had done to improve it. He spoke in a booming Afrikaans accent and peppered his sentences with, "You won't believe it!" with heavy emphasis always on the second word. Occasionally he would throw in a, "If you don't believe me you can ask my brother—I will take you to him!"

Most of what he was asking us to believe was the magnificence of a fence that he had erected on his farm. When we got there it was getting dark but he insisted on showing us the fence, and he threw the Land Rover off the track so that we could follow the line of the fence up hill and down dale. It was indeed a stout fence and it went on for miles but to listen to Henke it was the eighth wonder of the world. Steve and I were exhorted to gaze in admiration and wonderment as the vehicle trundled over the uneven terrain until it got so dark we could not even see it any more. Still Henke was not satisfied that we had seen enough and he switched on his lights so that we would not miss anything of his creation.

Back at the farmhouse, which he had renovated such that we "would not believe it," Henke chucked a few sausages on the indoor barbecue and made sandwiches. The wine amounted to a 50 cl bottle of cheap red for me, and Steve's beer was one can of Castle Light.

Henke explained that he didn't like to offer us more to drink, as he didn't know us "and some people get funny ways when they've had a drink."

The banquet might have been a bit light but he gave us a fascinating insight into the life of an Afrikaans farmer. He had inherited his farm from his father and it was huge, there were points where all you could see was owned by Henke. He was very proud of it and bragged ceaselessly about how big it was and how much it was worth. There really didn't seem to be much else in his life. However, his brother had the neighbouring farm and this was about ten times as big.

At first Henke spoke glowingly about his brother and how clever he was, but as the evening wore on, he got more and more bitter about the way his brother had "cheated him" out of his inheritance. Apparently, he was so rich that even his "boys" (his workers, not his sons), had cars but Henke claimed that he was obsessed by money and that "nobody liked him." Certainly Henke didn't.

When we first struck the deal with Henke, he promised to take us to the top of the mountain range which separated us from the Garden Route. However, each time he made a reference to this part of the deal, the distance which he was going to take us decreased. It went from the mountain top to the village at the bottom of the mountain and then became a village halfway there. Each time, Steve and I exchanged a knowing glance. In the event, he took us no farther than the end of the track from his farm to the main road, claiming that he had urgent business in the opposite direction. This time it was an old German proverb that was brought to mind: "Promises are like the full moon: if they are not kept at once they diminish day by day."

We had lost about twenty miles through his duplicity but neither of us would have missed the opportunity to meet such a colourful old rogue. Steve is a brilliant mimic and there were times when I almost fell off my bike laughing at some of his catch phrases, especially, "You won't believe it!" Naturally, from then on, we couldn't pass a fence without extolling its virtues in the most extravagant manner.

About a month later we rolled into the outskirts of Cape Town, where we stayed with some friends of Steve's, and the following morning we rode to City Hall which was our official journey's end. Cape Town is a lovely city and as a tourist resort is second to no city I have ever visited. Steve's friend Mark is a tour guide and he took us on a number of the excursions that no tourist should miss. In the space of a few days we did the Stellenbosch wine route, climbed Table Mountain, visited Robben Island and joined an official tour of a township in Cape Flats. It felt so odd to walk unafraid around a township when for so long I had been terrified at the sight of one. But then you would be terrified of a lion you meet in the wild but the same lion in a zoo, through no fault of its own, inspires only pity and contempt.

It takes about an hour and a half to walk up Table Mountain and I ascended in bright sunshine. The view across the city and the bay was magnificent but by the time I got to the top, the "table cloth," as the locals call the thick fog which often shrouds the summit, had come down. I couldn't see a thing, apart from the odd little furry creatures that live up there. I walked down again, soaked to the skin and damn cold. After eight months of cycling, I was amazed to find that the following day my legs had seized up after just three hours walking.

Much as I enjoyed Cape Town and its attractions, one of which is its unthreatening ambience, I was feeling very homesick, and I really wanted to go home. South African Airways sold me a one-way ticket home and I left Steve and Mark to cycle through the Cape Flats to the airport. On my own in the townships, I again felt the apprehension that was missing from the tour but decided that if I had to choose between fear and contempt, I would choose fear. It was more natural.

To my amazement the guy at check-in accepted my bike without a quibble and, having taken nine months to traverse Africa on a bike, I did the return journey by air in less than a day. The difference is, riding through Africa I had experiences I will never forget—I don't remember a damn thing about the flight home. I didn't see anything interesting, meet anyone interesting and I wasn' t even particularly terrified. Most importantly, my transportation (as well as my safety and comfort) was now in the hands of someone else. It was stage one of my resumption of normal life.

Chapter 15

I am glad to say that for a large part of my journey I was with other cyclists, I started with my friend Reg and finished with my brother Steve. In between I met cyclists of various nationalities and shared adventures with them all. I also met other travellers and along with all of them I tried to find some sense in the fantastic nonsense that is Africa. That I didn't succeed was not their fault or even my own—perhaps there just isn't any to find. Or perhaps I just failed to recognise it.

I never got around to actually listing the ten reasons why Africa will never win the World Cup but no doubt the first three are Corruption at the top, Corruption in the middle and Corruption at the bottom. To get a feel for how deep-rooted corruption is in Africa, all you have to do is watch a policeman taking his "gift" from a bus driver. Neither he nor his victim feels that it is in any way wrong, and that is what is so depressing. It is a disease that riddles the body of Africa.

Then there are the real diseases, principally malaria although AIDS seems to get all the publicity. Malaria kills about a million Africans every year, most of them children. It is getting worse because the drugs quickly become useless as the parasites mutate. Enough has already been said about AIDS in Africa. Certain vital drugs have become more available to some sufferers, and there is

BASIL JOHN MANDY

perhaps less of the weird thinking on the subject in government circles, but the epidemic just gets worse. Diarrhoea kills as many as malaria, largely because so many people do not have access to clean water. Excessive religiosity is a hindrance to progress all over Africa but especially in those countries just south of the Sahara, where forms of Christianity hold sway. In Nigeria, for example, over ninety-five percent of the population are practising Christians which, in effect, means everybody. But their faith is a strange, fundamentalist travesty of Christianity, as unpleasant and as intolerant as that found in the Bible belt of the Deep South in America. It is not too far removed from the cult of the witch doctor and his "muti." The poor willingly give their meagre possessions to the "church" and so stay poor while a few clerics become fabulously wealthy. Most people live in shanties without electricity and decent sanitation but the demand for huge new cathedrals seems to be insatiable.

Finding oil in Nigeria put untold wealth in the pockets of a few but led to more misery and blight for the majority. Greedy western corporations know they can rely on the self-interest of the African ruling classes. Now they have found oil in other African countries but there is nothing to suggest that the story will be any different.

In some countries, the IMF and the World Bank have got their claws into economic policy and in many ways this is as damaging as the old colonialism. They maintain their hold through the manipulation of national debt and the threat to withhold aid. The aid industry is massive in Africa, it employs more people than any other activity except government. It also leads to a dependency culture and an irrational reliance on outside agencies to solve problems. Any traveller in a third-world country will come across widespread begging and having spent some time in India, particularly Mumbai, I do not have a problem with it either in practice or in concept. But in Africa I detected a subtle difference: begging was acceptable at much higher levels of society. Trendy teenagers and expensively dressed business people often approached me with the open hand. As individuals and as nations there seems to be a zeitgeist that says it is OK to want something for nothing, to be dependent. Even leaders talk about Western aid as a right, in terms that you do not hear from governments of poor countries from other continents. Africans think only the West can solve their problems and aid agencies rush to reinforce that view.

Of course many of the problems are inter-related. From corruption comes crime, violence, political instability: from tribalism comes more corruption, hatred, fear. All over Southern Africa the blacks hate and resent the whites while the whites fear and mistrust the blacks. This is a phenomenon which seriously blighted my own journey through Africa. All my life I have despised racism but it was so powerful that, for a while, even I thought and behaved like a racist.

South Africa's "Rainbow Nation" lasted a few months and now nobody even mentions it. Nelson Mandela is seen by many black South Africans as a man who gives legitimacy and credence to a party, the ANC, that has failed dismally in many areas of governance. And this is probably the best government in Africa, the only one that has been democratically elected more than twice in succession.

I am not an economist or a sociologist but all these problems, and more, were plainly visible to me on my bike. Some are home-grown problems and some can be laid at the door of the West. What they all have in common is that they are getting worse not better. The greatest footballer who ever lived, Pele, was born into poverty but that didn't stop him leading his country to World Cup victory. Indeed Brazil have won it five times and that is a country well acquainted with crime, disease, poverty and many of the other problems found in Africa. So why can Brazil do with ease something which is impossible for an African country? Why will a country with no football heritage, like Japan or China, win the World Cup before an African country? I don't know what the answer is, just as I don't know why a continent which has been blessed with more riches and resources than any other should be mired so deeply in chaos, squalor and hatred. All I can suggest is that countries that are capable of winning a World Cup, or achieving success in any field of endeavour, have a collective sense of self worth and a respect for all their fellow citizens. They have confidence in the future and they instinctively believe that they are the best people to solve their own problems. Africans don't seem to share these traits and that is why Africa is not going forward and that is why I was so disappointed in the continent. And that is why I don't believe Africa will win the World Cup.

Printed in the United States
30324LVS00001B/64-111